ADVANCE PRAISE

"Carlos Reyes is quickly building a reputation as a talented and experienced RC model aircraft expert and author. His first book, titled *RCadvisor's Model airplane Design Made Easy*, set the stage for what I'm sure will be a series of books that will allow a rank beginner to get a start and then progress to any desired level in our wonderful hobby.

Carlos just introduced his second book under his RCadvisor.com publishing company, titled *RCadvisor's ModiFly*. The subtitle states, "Design and build from scratch your own modern flying model airplane in one day for just $5"! This new book will do just that in about 150 pages that are jammed with technical information that will allow a hobby newcomer to build from scratch and fly his first radio controlled model aircraft. The amount of detail is incredible and will certainly apply to many other aircraft that you build as you grow in the hobby. Carlos Reyes has a truly enjoyable style of writing—technical YES!—but also fun to read while you are learning so much at the same time!

This new book is excellent for any age group be they young or old. This is absolutely A MUST READ! I can only imagine (and look forward to) what book number three will be like!"

Bob Aberle, *AMA 215*
Technical Editor
Model Aviation *magazine*

"I would liken the latest book from Carlos Reyes to an experienced mentor inviting you to his workshop for a relaxed discussion on the whys and wherefores of how things are done. You are presented with a new model airpane design supported by a conversational discussion of the different factors that went into deriving the final configuration. Ideas that worked along with those that did not are presented with clear easy to understand explanations. Even if you have some model airplane design experience, you are likely to learn something from this book. I know I did."

Paul Bradley
Small Field Flying *Columnist*
Model Aviation *magazine*

"Carlos Reyes has done it again! He has written a book that clearly communicates the way to begin designing and scratch building RC airplanes. This hobby has a big learning curve to it, but his book makes it a lot easier to reach your goals. There is nothing more enjoyable than to design and build an aircraft with your own hands and see it flying successfully. This book will help you enjoy that rewarding experience."

Dick Kline
Author of The Ultimate Paper Airplane *book*
Kline Fogleman airfoil inventor

"I was really hoping Carlos' next book would be informative, entertaining, helpful, and have a brilliant educational aspect for RC flying hobbyists. However, this book didn't quite do this; it was *BEYOND* these expectations! Carlos kicks out another winner with this one. Yes, you can have entertaining and helpful media in RC other than podcasts!"

Jamie Burke
Host
`www.AllThingsThatFly.com`

"Carlos has captured the very essence of simplicity in the complex world of design. The simple approach built around understandable layman's terms will go a long way in encouraging and guiding anyone with a desire to learn the fine art of model airplane design."

Pat Tritle
Model Airplane Designer
`www.PatsCustom-Models.com`

"After demystifying much of the RC modeling hobby in his first book (*RCadvisor's Model Airplane Design Made Easy*), Carlos Reyes' latest endeavor walks us through the build of a low-cost and unique plane that anyone can manage. Lots of great info for the budding scratch builder in all of us!"

Michael "Crash" Hancock
Host
`www.TheCrashCast.com`

"This is Carlos' second book and builds on the knowledge gained in the first. Every school library should have these two books. Carlos takes you through the building steps and most importantly, he tells you why things do or don't work. Most only tell you how to do things, Carlos tells you why."

Greg Gimlick
Electrics *Columnist*
Model Aviation *magazine*

"This book picks up where Carlos' first book left off. Very informative for both beginners and experts. Great tips and ideas for even the most seasoned hobbyist. Many tricks I never thought of and have already incorporated into my own scratch building."

Frank Betts
Host
`www.RcFlightCast.com`

"For the vast majority of model airplane enthusiasts, the goal of the hobby can be encapsulated in one word, "fun". Fun doesn't require large expenditures of money. It doesn't require huge investments of time. Fun doesn't require high-tech materials. Whether you're a relative newcomer to radio controlled aircraft or a seasoned expert, this book will demonstrate how you can actually try something that's always been lurking in the back of your imagination. It can be easy, but, most of all, it can be a lot of fun."

Rocky S. Stone
38 years of modeling experience

"Carlos Reyes has produced this book to help those who are interested in building and flying model planes, but especially those who would like to design their own. These days there are many so-called Ready-To-Fly models available, many of them in toy stores. These have made learning to fly relatively simple, but there's nothing to equal the satisfaction that comes from creating your own plane and seeing it fly successfully.

The book, *RCadvisor's ModiFly*, provides the "know-how" to make that happen. It covers all the details involved, particularly in regard to building from foam sheets, rather than the traditional balsa wood. This is an important feature, because it's the wave of the present and the future.

The model featured in the book is not the most glamorous looking model, but it incorporates the simplest and soundest construction techniques necessary for successful design and flight. Carlos has made sure that nothing in the design and building process is taken for granted. He has devoted much attention to all the details that guide and guarantee that the learning process is complete and, if followed, will assure success."

John Worth
former President and Executive Director of the Academy of Model Aeronautics and currently Executive Editor of RC Micro World, *an online monthly magazine about the smallest and lightest of model aircraft:*
www.Cloud9Rc.com

"Invading the mind of a designer is an intriguing adventure. After reading just the first chapter about the goals, along with what did and didn't work on the prototypes, I was eager to read on to see how the modified design worked out. Carlos continues by explaining what considerations were used, and how they were derived, to pick a "Winner" from the many prototypes. I carefully studied Carlos' ideas and techniques and learned a lot about designing this type of plane. I am so excited about the design that I just have to build one to try it out."

Ken Myers
Editor
The Ampeer *electric flight newsletter of the Electric Flyers Only of Southeastern Michigan*
`http://homepage.mac.com/kmyersefo/`

"I really enjoyed reading *RCadvisor's ModiFly*. I'm going to build the model described in the book. I also like the design process described. It will help experienced designers as well as those just starting to scratch build."

Mark Johnston
Associate Vice President
AMA District 8

"What an excellent foray into model airplane practical design! This easy to build airplane design comes with loads of theory included for every design consideration. The section on symptoms and the causes of various flight characteristics or maladies is priceless information. Instructions on how to build the plane are very clear and there are many pictures making this book an excellent guide for educational uses. Every RC enthusiast could get something out of this book. Well done!"

Richard Chase
RC Heli Flight School Instructor
`www.IHeartHeli.com`

"There are an incredible number of decisions that you have to make when you design your own model airplane. This book is a great resource for helping make the right decisions. It's like having a seasoned model airplane designer around, telling you all the decisions (and mistakes!) that went into building his latest design."

Rick Witter
Engineer and Instrument-Rated Private Pilot

"Carlos' latest book, *RCadvisor's ModiFly*, is like a well written mystery novel. It introduces each design parameter, considers, and examines them in depth. Each decision step is carefully interrogated with the survivors then blended skillfully into the ModiFly design. A fun read that takes you inside the head of the writer as he examines and selects the optimum from a cost, form, and function standpoint from a myriad of materials and techniques to end up with an inexpensive and versatile model from which one can further experiment with his own ideas."

Red Scholefield
The *R/C Battery Clinic*
Model Aviation *Magazine*

RCadvisor's ModiFly

Design and Build From Scratch
Your Own Modern Flying Model Airplane
In One Day for Just $5

Carlos Reyes
www.RCadvisor.com founder

RCadvisor.com
Albuquerque, New Mexico

Copyright © 2009 by Carlos Reyes. All rights reserved.

No part of this book may be reproduced in any form or by any electronic or mechanical means including information storage and retrieval systems, without permission in writing from the author. The only exception is by a reviewer, who may quote short excerpts in a review.

Published by:
RCadvisor.com
2200 Elizabeth St NE
Albuquerque, NM 87112-3037
1-505-206-1569
`carlos@rcadvisor.com`

ISBN 978-0-9822613-4-7

Library of Congress Control Number: 2009905988

Library of Congress subject headings:
Airplanes—Models—Design and construction.
Airplanes—Models—Aerodynamics.
Airplanes—Models—Radio control.

Cover design by Tammy Crespin. Book design by Carlos Reyes. Typeset using the amazing LaTeX system.

This paper meets the requirements of ANSI/NISO Z39.48-1992 (Permanence of Paper).

Version 1.0

To Tammy,
the wind beneath my wings.

Summary Table of Contents

Preface		23
1	**Design Process**	27
2	**The Winner**	43
3	**Prepare to Build**	63
4	**Building**	73
5	**Flying**	127
6	**Enhancements**	131
7	**Variations**	135
8	**Make It Your Own!**	139
Index		141
Colophon		147

Contents

Preface — 23

1 Design Process — 27
- 1.1 Why Yet Another Design — 27
- 1.2 Goals — 27
  - 1.2.1 A Starting Point for Other Designs — 28
  - 1.2.2 Easy to Build — 28
  - 1.2.3 Inexpensive — 29
  - 1.2.4 Sound Technical Design — 29
- 1.3 Ungoals — 30
  - 1.3.1 Sexy Looks — 30
  - 1.3.2 Wild Performance — 30
  - 1.3.3 Technology Showcase — 30
- 1.4 Preliminary Design — 31
  - 1.4.1 Power System — 31
  - 1.4.2 Size — 31
  - 1.4.3 Materials — 31
  - 1.4.4 Aerodynamics — 32
- 1.5 Prototyping Process — 32
  - 1.5.1 Test Flying — 33
  - 1.5.2 Flight Testing Quiz — 34
- 1.6 Rejected Ideas — 37

2 The Winner — 43

2.1	Cost		43
2.2	Structural Components		45
	2.2.1	Wing	45
	2.2.2	Tail	47
	2.2.3	Fuselage	47
	2.2.4	Control Surfaces	48
	2.2.5	Motor Mount	49
2.3	Power System		49
	2.3.1	RCadvisor's Calculator	51
	2.3.2	Field Testing Tools	56
2.4	Radio Components		58
2.5	Lessons Learned		58
2.6	Specifications		59

3 Prepare to Build 63
3.1	Materials		63
	3.1.1	Foamboard	63
	3.1.2	Dowels	64
	3.1.3	Piano Wire	65
	3.1.4	Control Horns	66
	3.1.5	Hinge Tape	66
	3.1.6	Craft Sticks	67
	3.1.7	Masking Tape	67
3.2	Adhesives		67
	3.2.1	Laminating Glue	67
	3.2.2	Structural Glue	68
	3.2.3	Glue Safety	69
3.3	Required Tools		69
	3.3.1	Cutting and Drilling Tools	69
	3.3.2	Sanding Tools	70
	3.3.3	Measuring and Marking Tools	70
3.4	Optional Tools		70
3.5	Work Area		71

4 Building   73
4.1 Make Kit Parts 73
4.1.1 Mark Foam Parts 75
4.1.2 Cut Foam Parts 75
4.1.3 Remove Paper 75
4.1.4 Cut Dowels 80
4.2 Vertical Stabilizer 80
4.2.1 Mark Lines 80
4.2.2 Cut Hinge 83
4.2.3 Cut Rudder Bevel 83
4.2.4 Tape Hinge 88
4.2.5 Cut Round Corners 88
4.2.6 Mount Control Horn 91
4.2.7 Glue on Supports 94
4.2.8 Sand Edges 95
4.3 Horizontal Stabilizer 95
4.3.1 Mark Lines 95
4.3.2 Cut Hinge 97
4.3.3 Tape Hinge 97
4.3.4 Cut Round Corners 99
4.3.5 Sand Edges 99
4.4 Wing 99
4.4.1 Mark Lines 100
4.4.2 Cut Ailerons 101
4.4.3 Tape Ailerons 101
4.4.4 Laminate Bottom Step 101
4.4.5 Glue Main Spar and Wing Support 103
4.4.6 Glue Leading Edge Spar 103
4.4.7 Cut Round Corners 104
4.4.8 Sand the Edges 104
4.5 Fuselage 104
4.5.1 Glue Dowels to Top Foam Piece 104
4.5.2 Add the Triangular Supports 106

		4.5.3	Affix Motor Mount Supports	106

        4.5.3   Affix Motor Mount Supports 106
        4.5.4   Finish with Side Foam Pieces and Bottom Dowel . . 110
  4.6   Motor Mount 110
        4.6.1   Cut and Glue Pieces 110
        4.6.2   Drill Holes 111
        4.6.3   Glue on Fuselage 111
  4.7   Final Assembly 111
        4.7.1   Painting and Decorating 111
        4.7.2   Glue on Wing and Horizontal Stabilizer 111
        4.7.3   Mount Elevator Control Horn 118
        4.7.4   Mount Aileron Control Horns 118
        4.7.5   Glue on Vertical Stabilizer 118
        4.7.6   Attach Motor 118
        4.7.7   Attach Propeller 119
  4.8   Radio Installation 119
        4.8.1   Tape on Tail Servos 119
        4.8.2   Tape on Aileron Servos 122
        4.8.3   Tape on Receiver and Speed Control 122
        4.8.4   Velcro the Battery 124
        4.8.5   Radio Programming 124

5 Flying   127
  5.1   The Right Place and Time 127
  5.2   Preflight 127
  5.3   Toss It 128
  5.4   Repairs 130
  5.5   Extended Test Flying 130

6 Enhancements   131
  6.1   Painting and Decorating 131
  6.2   Removable Wing 132
  6.3   Landing Gear 133
  6.4   Sorta Scale 133

6.5	Camera Plane	133

7 Variations   135
7.1	Free Flight Glider	135
7.2	Basic Trainer	136
7.3	Slow Flyer	136
7.4	Sloper	136
7.5	Combat	136
7.6	Pylon Racer	137
7.7	Motorglider	137
7.8	3D Aerobat	137

8 Make It Your Own!   139

Index   141

Colophon   147

About the Author	147
RCadvisor's Calculator	147
Website	150
This Book	150

List of Figures

2.1	Rejected Prototypes	44
2.2	Paper Airplane	48
2.3	Airplane at Cruise	52
2.4	Power System at Cruise	54
2.5	Airplane at Maximum Speed	55
2.6	Airplane Stall Speed	56
2.7	Motor at Maximum Power	57
4.1	Mark Foam Parts	76
4.2	Cut Foam Parts	77
4.3	Remove Paper	78
4.4	Using Tweezers to Remove Paper	79
4.5	Cut Dowels	81
4.6	Airplane Mock-up	82
4.7	Mark V Stab Lines	84
4.8	Prepare to Cut Rudder Hinge	85
4.9	Cut Rudder Hinge	86
4.10	Cut Rudder Bevel	87
4.11	Tape Rudder Hinge Side 1	88
4.12	Tape Rudder Hinge Side 2	89
4.13	Round Vert Stab Corners	90
4.14	Control Horns	91
4.15	Control Horn Holes	92
4.16	Control Horn Slot	93

4.17	Rudder Control Horn Side View	93
4.18	Vert Stab Side Supports	94
4.19	Vert Stab Side Supports Mounted	96
4.20	Horiz Stab Marked Lines	97
4.21	Horiz Stab Hinge Cutting	98
4.22	Completed Horiz Stab	99
4.23	Marking Lines on Wing	100
4.24	Wing Reinforcement	102
4.25	Wing Lamination	103
4.26	Wing Main Spar	104
4.27	Wing Leading Edge	105
4.28	Completed Wing	106
4.29	Fuselage Top	107
4.30	Fuselage Support Triangles	108
4.31	Fuselage Support Triangles Glued On	108
4.32	Fuselage Nose	109
4.33	Fuselage Sides	110
4.34	Motor Mount	112
4.35	Motor Mount on Fuselage	113
4.36	Hand Painted Wing	114
4.37	Hand Painted Fuselage	115
4.38	Glue on Wing and Horiz Stab	116
4.39	Glue on Horiz Stab	117
4.40	Motor Mount Washers	120
4.41	Taping Down Rudder Servo	121
4.42	Taping Down Aileron Servos	123
4.43	Radio Components	125
5.1	Launching	129
8.1	Carlos Reyes	148
8.2	RCadvisor's calculator	149

List of Tables

2.1	Actual Cost	45
2.2	Power System Components	50
2.3	Summary Specs	60
2.4	Wing Specs	60
2.5	Fuselage Specs	61
2.6	Horizontal Stabilizer Specs	61
2.7	Vertical Stabilizer Specs	61
3.1	Required Supplies	64
3.2	Actual Dowel Sizes	65
4.1	Foam Parts	74
4.2	Dowel Parts	74

Preface

How does an original model airplane design get created?

I've always wanted to read a book that answered that question. A book that takes me by the hand and shows me how it's really done. One that tells me not just the what and the how, but also the all important why. Since nobody had ever written such a book, I decided to do it myself. This is that book.

My first book, *RCadvisor's Model Airplane Design Made Easy*, quickly became a bestseller. It was a real joy to write it. I've also derived a lot of pleasure from the many emails readers have sent me describing how much they've enjoyed reading it.

I view that book as a precursor to this one. Reading that book first is not required, but doing so will greatly enhance the learning experience.

I am also the founder of the RCadvisor[1] website, which contains an advanced free online calculator for model airplane design and building. As with my previous book, having access to the calculator will enhance the learning experience but is not a prerequisite.

Overview of the book

This book describes in detail the creation process of a specific model airplane. It is designed to be read in sequence.

The focus is on the practical application of aerodynamic theory. The goal is not to make general statements but instead to have an in-depth discussion of a specific design.

---

[1] www.RCadvisor.com

As with my previous book, I've attempted to cover the needs of a global audience. Both U.S. customary and metric units of measure are given where appropriate and practical.

Disclaimers

This book is designed to provide information on designing, building and flying model aircraft. It is sold with the understanding that the publisher and author are not involved in rendering professional services. If expert assistance is required, the services of a competent professional should be sought.

It is not the purpose of this book to reprint all the information that is otherwise available, but instead to complement, amplify and supplement other information sources.

Trademarked names are used throughout this book. We are using the names only in an editorial fashion. The usage is to the benefit of the trademark owners and there is no intention to infringe on their legal rights.

Every effort has been made to make this book as complete and accurate as possible. However, I am not perfect. This book may contain both typographical and content errors.

The purpose of this book is to educate and entertain. The author and RCadvisor.com shall have neither liability nor responsibility to any person or entity with respect to any loss or damage caused, or alleged to have been caused, directly or indirectly, by the information contained in this book.

Acknowledgments

I have not attempted to cite in the text the authorities and sources consulted in the preparation of this book. To do so would require more space than is available.

I am incredibly lucky to have an amazing group of talented reviewers. They've all given generously of their time to make this book even better. You can find their comments at the beginning of the book.

In addition, I want to give special thanks to Ken Myers, Richard Chase, Rick Witter, Rocky Stone, and Tammy Crespin. The book is much improved because of their extensive feedback. Thank you.

Carlos

1 Design Process

Designing a model airplane is a lot of fun. To me, it's like a big jigsaw puzzle. The pieces appear to fit together many different ways. You can even force them together any which way, but it won't be pretty. There's is only one "best" way to assemble the puzzle, and it can take many tries to find it.

1.1 Why Yet Another Design

Why not? There are an infinite number of possible designs. With the right set of goals and constraints, I knew I had a good shot at coming up with an interesting and unique design.

1.2 Goals

A well-defined set of goals with a tight set of constraints are key to encouraging the creation of an innovative design.

Let's face it. It doesn't take a genius to put together a flyable design given today's composite materials, lightweight radio gear, brushless motors, and LiPo batteries. Almost anything will fly.

I knew I needed a detailed list of constraints, but I also didn't want to design against an arbitrary set of requirements. They had to make sense and they had to lead to an interesting, useful model.

1.2.1 A Starting Point for Other Designs

The primary goal for the design was always clear. It was to provide a starting point in the book for other designs. There are many implications behind this simple statement.

This automatically ruled out exotic configurations such as a pusher, canard or flying wing. It had to be a conventional configuration design that could be easily molded into other shapes.

Exotic or hard to find materials were also out. I have a stack of top-quality pultruded carbon rods in my workshop that I got at a great price. They are normally hard to find and expensive. Sorry, but I just couldn't use them.

Advanced tools, such as hot wire foam cutters, vacuum bagging equipment, or CNC foam cutters were definitely out. These all require special equipment that most modelers do not have. I even avoided requiring common equipment such as a drill or Dremel rotary tool.

The model had to be fun to fly with no bad habits. If it flew like a dog, then who would want to have anything to do with it?

Reasonably good crash resistance became an early goal. Too many test flights don't end well. My goal was to help others, not frustrate them.

It had to be an easily malleable design, maintaining the pleasant flight characteristics even with build errors and ill-conceived design modifications. This is a difficult goal to measure and even harder to achieve.

What different variations could I accommodate? I wanted to make sure I did not rule out reasonable design modifications that others might want to build. Slope flyer, motorglider, free flight model, trainer, park flyer, indoor slow flyer, etc. were all within the scope.

1.2.2 Easy to Build

This is arguably a goal of any model airplane design. I expanded the definition to make it clear what I meant.

Only use tools, glues, and materials that most readers would be able to find locally. Don't assume that a hobby shop is nearby. This constraint really limited my choices.

No hard to master techniques. This ruled out, for example, hot melt glues and spray adhesives. I've managed to totally mess up models I've tried to build with both.

To me, easy to build also implies no toxic materials or adhesives. If I want to build with my bare hands and spread out the glue with my fingers, I should be able to do so without serious danger to my health.

Buildable in a day was not an explicit goal, but after a few design iterations it became very achievable.

1.2.3 Inexpensive

I made this a goal because I felt that I could still put together a great design even if I only used very inexpensive materials.

The easy to build and inexpensive goals had a synergistic effect. What if you could build the airplane in one day for less than $5? All of a sudden, trying out a new design variation became a lot more practical. With so little invested in each airplane built, I became a lot more adventurous in the changes I was willing to try. This is a key point—don't underestimate it's value.

It goes without saying that the $5 covers the cost of the airplane itself, not the motor or radio components. I don't have much control over those. If you build it as a free flight glider, then $5 covers everything. In a crash, the airplane is much more likely to break than the other expensive parts. With careful shopping, an appropriate power system and on-board radio system can be purchased for about $100.

1.2.4 Sound Technical Design

Beyond all of the above, I wanted to be able to justify every design decision made. Every feature of the design needed to be traceable to either aerodynamic theory or flight testing results. This is a much higher bar than the typical design, but I felt justified in enforcing it.

This was harder to do than I anticipated. I had to question every material and construction technique I used. It was very tempting to just accept the research of others, but I just couldn't do that. I tried many variations to make sure I was using the best materials and techniques. In some cases, I was very surprised to learn that a base assumption I had made was very wrong.

1.3 Ungoals

Equally important was the list of goals I wasn't going to pursue. It really helps a lot to spell these out. It stops feature creep dead on its tracks. The designs are much less compromised, opening the door for an innovation breakthrough like I experienced.

1.3.1 Sexy Looks

Sorry! Sexy good looks were never a design goal. I was going for more of a plain vanilla look. Something that could later be modified and spiced up as desired.

Similarly, I decided not to pursue any kind of scale appearance. Not needed and not wanted. Easy enough to work it into the design later.

1.3.2 Wild Performance

Good performance was always a goal, but unlimited aerobatics or 3D flying never was. Nothing prevents the design from being enhanced later. As it turned out, the model is a very decent aerobatic flyer. But that was strictly a bonus and not a specific design goal.

1.3.3 Technology Showcase

I did not want to rely on any gimmicks or bleeding edge technologies to achieve my goals. Everything had to be mainstream. Only mature technologies need apply.

1.4 Preliminary Design

What options did I have left after all the constraints and restrictions? Quite a few, as it turned out.

1.4.1 Power System

This one was a no-brainer for me. To keep costs down, I knew it was going to be a small model. That meant either a park flyer or indoor model, both of which screamed electric power. This meant using mainstream technologies such as brushless outrunner electric motors and lithium polymer (LiPo) cells.

1.4.2 Size

I knew I'd be building and crashing a few prototypes during the development process. What was the least expensive size to target?

After studying a few retailer websites and catalogs, it became clear that the pricing of motors, servos, and speed controllers generally went down until a certain point. Then their prices either stabilized or started going back up.

Doing some quick calculations, I learned that the price sweet spot was at around a model flying weight of six ounces (170 grams).

I have to add that the pricing situation of the micro components is dramatically better than it was just a couple of years ago. Who knows where we'll be in a couple more years? Regardless, I was designing a model for today.

The target weight turned out to have a major unexpected bonus: it opened the door to having both indoor slow flyer and park flyer design variations.

1.4.3 Materials

The decision to use foam as the primary construction material was an easy one. It is very inexpensive, consistent in quality and easy to work with. There is no better inexpensive source of high quality foam than foamboard.

I always remove the paper that is attached to both sides of the foamboard. It adds to the strength, but it also adds a lot to the weight, doubling it.

Spruce for model use is overrated. I prefer plain hardwood dowels and sticks. They are very inexpensive and work great as reinforcements. Similarly, craft sticks come in handy for building motor mounts and such.

1.4.4 Aerodynamics

The Reynolds number is used to make predictions about the behavior of air as it goes past an airplane wing. It depends mainly on the speed of the airplane and the chord size of the wing.

A slow small model meant low Reynolds numbers. For the best efficiency, the airfoil needed to be 6% thick or less.

I wanted a really easy to build airfoil, which led me quickly to the Kline--Fogleman (KFm) airfoil family. These airfoils are similar to flat plates in appearance, but offer significantly better performance.

A more cambered airfoil would have probably yielded better performance. But I could not see a way to do this and maintain the ease of building and strength.

For flying in small fields and indoors, the wing loading needed to be low. Because of the low wing loading, I was concerned at first about flying outdoors in wind. As it turned out, I need not have been concerned.

An interesting question became the target pilot skill level. At first I thought of building a trainer. Then I realized that scratch builders probably have experience with other models. My goal became the design of a sport model. In truth, the final design has such pleasant flying qualities that it can serve as a trainer as well.

1.5 Prototyping Process

I wrote down some numbers and drew some sketches. After spending a few days thinking about my design, I knew it was time to start building prototypes and trying out my ideas.

1.5.1 Test Flying

Testing the early prototypes was tough. I crashed *a lot*. At the beginning all the flights lasted for less than five seconds. Invariably something in the model would break after one of these short flights, sending me back home for repairs. Sad.

It took me a while to sort it all out, and I slowly learned that there were many reasons why my models were test flying so poorly. The goal of this section is not to discourage you from trying to design your own model airplane. I sincerely hope that you will learn from my many mistakes and not follow the exact same road I did.

The first problem was the pilot. I had never flown a model in this size range. Even finding models in an R/C flight simulator that were similar to mine was very hard. I don't know anybody near me with experience with very small sport park flyers. I own a ParkZone[1] Vapor, and practicing with it did help some.

I also had no experience as a test pilot with problems of this magnitude. I've maidened models before, but other than trim changes, they always flew great from the get go. I'll be honest—my early prototypes were pretty much unflyable.

Compounding the lack of test pilot experience was my models' lack of crashworthiness. I made some dumb structural design decisions while putting the early versions together.

At first my prototypes suffered from trim issues, lack of control authority, and poor stability. Good luck trying to sort it all out when your model has three serious aerodynamic problems, all interacting with each other.

Talk about a recipe for disaster. Even if through some miracle I managed to make a decent landing, the structural design of the models was so poor that something usually broke, anyway.

I can laugh about it now, but I went through the cycle so many times, I mastered the art of the 30 minute test flying session: 10 minutes to drive

---

[1] www.parkzone.com

to the field, 10 minutes at the field, 10 minutes to drive back with my tail between my legs.

The lesson here should be obvious. Do everything you can to lower the number of unknowns. Try to find a model similar to what you are prototyping and make sure you can fly it well. Fly lots of different models, even if on a flight simulator.

The good news is that practice does make perfect. I maidened a new prototype twice a week for a couple of months. I got very good at doing a hand toss and then reacting very quickly to whatever happened next.

1.5.2 Flight Testing Quiz

Think you are a hot-shot pilot? That doesn't necessarily mean that you are a hot-shot airplane designer. Here are some situations I came across during my flight testing. What do you think are the causes of the problems?

The model flies fine, but when you cut the power the nose just drops.

This is a classic case of needing more downthrust. What is happening is that the motor is pulling the nose of the airplane up. To compensate, you dial in down elevator to level out the model at cruise. When you cut the power, all that down elevator takes over and just pulls the nose down.

Sometimes when gliding, the nose oscillates left and right.

Undamped yaw oscillations are caused by not enough dynamic stability. The easiest solution is to increase the size of the vertical stabilizer. Before you do that, though, ask yourself if this is a serious enough problem. If the problem only occurred once and the model was still perfectly controllable, then it might be fine to leave it as it is.

1 Design Process

The model either dives into the ground or stalls.

This should be an easy one to figure out. The center of gravity (CG or the balance point of the model) is too far back.

Most models benefit from a generous amount of pitch stability. Pattern airplanes need to impress the judges with their steady and smooth maneuvers. Large control surfaces and lots of stability are the rule.

One major exception is model thermalling gliders. Flying them with a rear CG and pitch sensitive lets the model respond easily to passing thermals. Finding thermals (or rising currents of air) is a critical task for these gliders.

When hit by a gust, the wings rock back and forth once or twice before settling down.

Increasing the dynamic roll stability will cure this problem. Easiest way is to increase the wing dihedral or sweep. But could it have just been too gusty? Did you have a reasonable expectation for rock solid stability under the flying conditions?

The wings bend quite a bit when you loop.

Is the model supposed to be able to loop? By itself, flexibility is not a problem.

Years ago I owned and flew regularly an ASW-20 full-size glider. Built around 1980, it was one of the last competition class sailplanes that did not make use of carbon fiber. It was all fiberglass. My friends would always tell me how the wings bent up dramatically every time I lifted off. The wings were very flexible, but the flying qualities were not affected.

If the model becomes uncontrollable because of all the flopping around, then it's definitely a problem. But some flexing is natural and should not be a concern.

After a crash you notice that the motor mount has broken off.

Was it a mild crash? Was it reasonable for the motor mount to break off? What actually broke—the glue, the wood, or the foam? Was it a freak accident? What's the pattern?

Everything in a design is a compromise. A model with a motor mount that never breaks is a model that's too heavy. You need to decide what is a reasonable trade-off between strength and weight.

When cruising around, the model flies with the nose high.

The wing incidence, or the angle that the wing makes in relation to the fuselage centerline, determines the attitude of the fuselage as the model flies around. I wouldn't worry about this if it's just a couple of degrees. A very nose high attitude at normal flying speeds should be fixed by repositioning the angle of the wing at the wing mount.

If the wing is too small, the model might be struggling to generate enough lift. You are flying around with too much induced drag. In that case a bigger wing is the better solution.

When you pull the nose up to do a loop, the model just stalls.

The model doesn't have enough inertia to carry it through the loop. You may need to dive to get the loop started. The problem could also be a lack of sufficient elevator travel.

Some full-size airplanes were designed with limited elevator travel on purpose. One of these airplanes was the Ercoupe, a small 2-seat airplane first manufactured in 1939. In an attempt to increase the safety of small airplanes, the designer made it unstallable by reducing the throw of the elevator.

Power off, aileron effectiveness drops dramatically.

The air being blown back by the propeller normally does wonders to the responsiveness of most models. It could just be that the control surfaces are too small or need more throw.

The downward-moving aileron can create a lot of drag, which pulls the nose in the direction opposite from that desired. This is called adverse yaw. This decreases the effectiveness of the ailerons. Using aileron differential, where the aileron that goes up is deflected more, is a common solution.

Sometimes the cause of the problem is too much aileron flexibility when you use a single centrally-located servo. The center section of the aileron deflects, but the rest just bends back into the airstream. Stiffen those suckers!

There are many ways of doing this. Strapping or hinge tape along the length of the aileron works fine. Rather than wrapping the tape around the trailing edge, I've found that it works better if the tape is just placed flat against one side of the aileron.

The model flies fine at cruise power, but becomes uncontrollable at high throttle.

Not enough downthrust can cause this. The nose goes up too much for the elevator to be able to compensate.

It can also be due to too much flexibility in the model. At high speed it starts bending and the control surfaces cannot keep up. Throttle back, bring it down, and investigate.

1.6 Rejected Ideas

After much grief and perseverance, I slowly built-up a list of ideas that had not worked out as hoped for.

Kline-Fogleman 2 Airfoil

This one turned out to be a long frustrating experience. I have studied all the research reports involving the KFm airfoils. After careful consideration, I selected the KFm2 airfoil (50% step on top) as the best choice for my model.

After a long trial and error process, I concluded that it's happiest with a CG at 70% of the chord. That is very far back! A normal airfoil has a CG at about 30%. This was odd, but I was prepared to live with it.

Then I noticed that it needed a lot of wing incidence, perhaps 8.5°. That is again huge, but I could live with it, too.

The clincher was the large amount of motor downthrust required, perhaps 12°. Being off by even a small amount caused no end of troubles. This was too problematic to ignore.

Flight testing a KFm1 airfoil (40% step on bottom) yielded a very pleasant flying airplane with none of the bad habits of the other KFm variant. I decided that there was no reason to put up with the KFm2, when the KFm1 was clearly much better.

For a long time I wondered if the strange behavior of the KFm2 was somehow due to some quirk in my design. After a lot of online searching I confirmed the 70% CG position. Then I came across a report of another model similar to mine that had the same problem with downthrust. What a relief!

These discoveries also confirmed a suspicion that I've had for a long time. Most designs published on the Internet have not been tested very well. The designs I came across with these problems are very popular, yet these aerodynamic quirks are barely known within their respective communities.

You could argue I lost out on one nice flying quality, but I beg to differ. You see, the KFm2 is unstallable. The model just sits there, nose pointed way up. The sink rate is correspondingly huge, but at least there is no sudden nose drop. The KFm1 can be made to stall if abused. The stall is very gentle and predictable. I don't see a problem with it, and it opened up the flight envelope to some new maneuvers.

What about the other KFm variants? Given the very low Reynolds number that my model flies at, the other variations did not look like a good fit since they are thicker.

EPP, EPS and Insulating Foams

Expanded polypropylene (EPP) was rejected because of cost since I don't have any local sources. I'd expect most builders to have to buy it via mail order, which makes it a lot more expensive. I also don't like the way it has to be extensively reinforced.

White beaded foam (expanded polystyrene foam or EPS) is very weak. I don't see that it offers any advantages over the alternatives.

I built a model with a fuselage out of Dow BlueCore insulating foam. It was a disappointment—heavy and relatively weak. At the time, I was using a contact cement for attaching the Velcro. Well, it just ate through the foam.

Depron and Cellfoam 88 were rejected because of cost. I knew I had a much less expensive source for high quality extruded polystyrene (XPS).

Plywood Motor Mount

Over time my motor mount went through six major design changes. I started by building them out of thin aircraft plywood. They worked great, but I was using a rotary tool to cut them out and to shape them. This was a dependency that I wanted to eliminate.

Strapping Tape

Strapping tape is the duct tape of the foam model airplane world. It gets used all over the airframes. As time went on, I used more and more of it in my prototypes. It is an easy fix for strength/stiffness problems.

I finally stepped back and thought it through. Polypropylene (PP), the material that it is made out of, actually has very poor stiffness by weight. Common hardwoods are about 20 times better. These woods are also about five times stronger by weight. All of a sudden, using strapping tape as a major structural component made no sense.

There's another problem with it. PP is a lightweight, tough, and very chemically inert material. Coroplast[2] is also made out of this.

---

[2] www.coroplast.com

Strong adhesives generally work by creating a chemical bond with the material that is being glued. Because PP does not react with most chemicals, it is almost impossible to get a strong glue joint to strapping tape or Coroplast. This was a headache that I could do without.

Removable Wing

In theory the idea of having removable wings sounded great. Build one fuselage and swap in different wings to get a rudder-only trainer or indoor slow flyer. Easier to transport, too.

In practice, the removable wing didn't work so well. The wing attachment posts were always coming loose. The mounting system added extra weight to the model and was another failure point. The clincher was the need to reprogram the radio when I switched from rudder-only to aileron ship. I was always afraid that I'd leave out a step in the switchover procedure. In the end, I just decided that it wasn't worth the hassle. For such a small and affordable airplane, it's easier to just build multiple airplanes with different wings permanently attached.

Velcro for Receiver and Speed Control

At one point I thought that attaching the receiver and speed control using hook and loop fasteners was a good idea. I figured that would give me more flexibility as I adjusted the balance point. But given that the receiver and speed control are so light, that makes little sense.

Of course, some pilots are short on components and want to swap the receiver, speed control, and battery between different airplanes. In that case, it makes perfect sense to use Velcro on all three.

Polyurethane Adhesives

I started out by liking the expanding polyurethane glues a lot. Originally sold as Gorilla glue, they are now found under a large variety of brand names such as Sumo glue and Elmer's Ultimate glue.

These are relatively fast drying, hold great, and are non-toxic. Wearing gloves is recommended while using them because they can stain fingers, especially the brown varieties.

The way they expand as they dry is their Achilles' heel. No matter how carefully you glue the joint, the glue expansion always makes your work look really sloppy. Sometimes, despite my best efforts, the expanding glue would shift the pieces being glued. I found that unacceptable.

Wing Taper, Sweep, Twist and Dihedral

I built wing variations with taper, sweep, and/or dihedral. In the end, I rejected all of that in favor of a simple and sturdy wing design.

I try to avoid designing wings with big heavy dihedral braces right at the centerline. A flat wing with sweep can be cut out of a single piece of foam, but then the spar will either be in a suboptimal location or will need to have a joint in it. There's a similar problem if I add a leading edge spar. Tapering the wing adds a similar complication.

The model looks like it needs dihedral, but it actually flies fine without it. Having a large fuselage side area, especially at the tail, helps a lot.

My earlier wings didn't have any wood reinforcements and were very light. Gusts would easily cause the model wings to rock back and forth. But the extra weight of the wood spars steadied them considerably.

Adding wing twist was never a good option. It's too hard to do reliably with a flat piece of foam. With a rectangular wing planform, it wasn't needed. Stalls always begin at the wing root.

Similarly, bending the foam to form an airfoil shape was also not seriously considered. That is a workable option with the insulating foams, but most other foams are just too brittle.

2 The Winner

Carrying out an experiment, studying the results, and following-up with another experiment is the key to innovation in any field. It was also common for me to build the model a certain way a dozen or more times before I would realize that there was a better approach.

In all, I built about 20 prototypes, each incorporating half a dozen or so design changes. By that estimate, I test flew well over 100 design variations. According to the cumulative timer on my transmitter, I flew them for a total of 15 hours (see Figure 2.1 on the following page).

That is a lot of experimentation and flight testing. Far more than the typical model airplane design gets. My goal was creating a breakthrough design, and I believe I achieved it.

This is the design I liked the most. I'm very happy with it. I hope you like it, too.

2.1 Cost

I added up the typical costs of the materials needed to build one airplane (see Table 2.1 on page 45). I'm sure these numbers will be obsolete the minute I write them down, but it's a good ballpark estimate. The total is comfortably below $5, and with bulk or discount purchases, it will be much less.

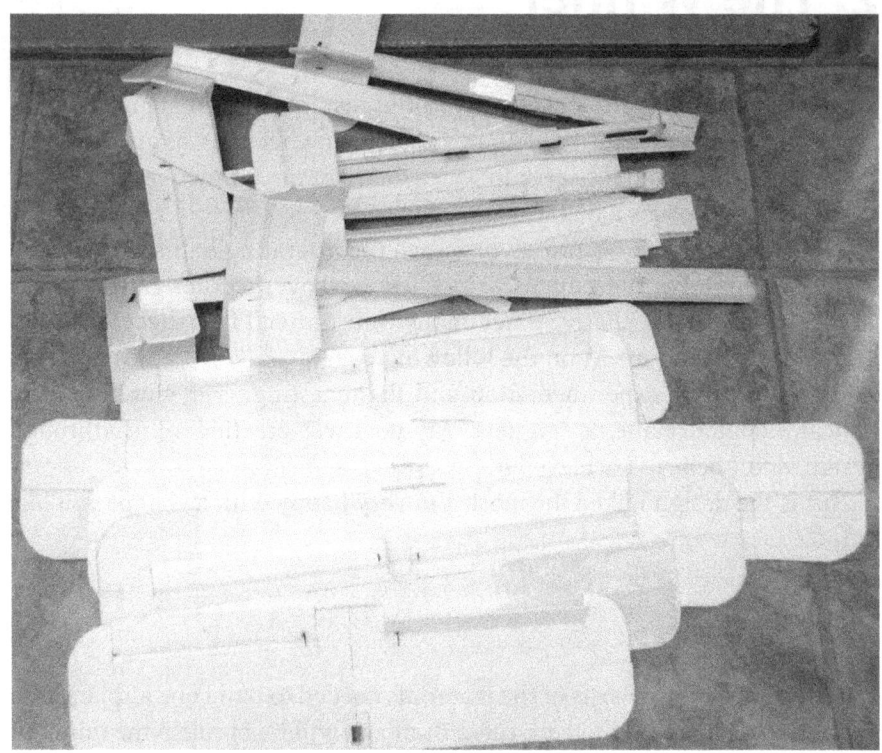

Figure 2.1 Rejected Prototypes
Some of my rejected prototypes.

Material	Cost ($)	Quantity Used	Total ($)
Foamboard	1.00	1	1.00
Dowels	0.29	5	1.45
Piano wire	0.50	1	0.50
Glue stick	2.00	1/10	0.20
Structural glue	2.50	1/10	0.25
Hinge tape	2.00	1/2	1.00
Nylon tie	2.00	1/15	0.13
Craft sticks	4.00	1/500	0.01
TOTAL			$4.54

Table 2.1 Actual Cost

2.2 Structural Components

2.2.1 Wing

A regular sized sheet of foamboard is 20 by 30 inches (51 by 76 cm) and about 0.175 inches (0.44 cm) thick with the paper removed. I didn't want any joints in the foam, so that set the size limit. The wing span became 30 inches.

From day one I knew that this was going to be a very low Reynolds number model. At these Reynolds numbers, a wing thickness of 6% or less is needed to delay separation in the air flow. That became my target thickness. If the wing was going to be two sheets of foam glued together for the KFm1 airfoil, then that meant that the chord should be about 6 inches (15 cm). With a 30 inch (76 cm) wingspan, that gave me a wing area of about 176 inches squared (1,135 sq cm) once you take into account the rounded corners.

Given the above constraints, the aspect ratio took care of itself. I got lucky and ended up with a nice middle of the road value (5.1). It gave me decent efficiency and structural strength.

What if the aspect ratio had been way outside the range that I wanted?

I would have had to decide what part of the design was more important and adjust it accordingly. All designs involve trade-offs. I would have loved to be able to include more camber in the wing, but doing so would have complicated the build and dramatically lowered the top speed.

The KFm1 and KFm2 airfoils are reported to work best at thicknesses of 7 to 9%. But 6% is not far from that range and my flight testing showed that they still work fine when thinned slightly.

The airplane type constant is related to the airplane weight, wing area, and wing span. It is useful for comparing the handling qualities of different airplanes.

The airplane type constant of the model is 0.00142. This is a low value, similar to what you'll find in a trainer like a Sig Kadet 40. Yet because of the thin airfoil, penetration into wind is excellent and far better than what you'd expect from a model this small.

The balance point of the model is about 33% of the way back from the nose on the fuselage. Since this is strongly influenced by the weight of the motor and battery, it will take some experimentation to find the right spot in a different design. A trick I used in some of the prototypes was to finish building the fuselage (including mounting the motor and radio components), find its CG without the wing, and then mounting the wing there.

Most of my models had no wing reinforcement at all. I rarely damaged a wing in a landing. But then I realized that the flexibility in the wings was messing up the flying qualities. I tried different reinforcement variations, finally settling on a small dowel for the main spar and a similar dowel on the leading edge for stiffness and crash resistance.

I flew one prototype with square corners on the wing and an unsanded leading edge. The handling was not quite as nice. The stall was sharper, for example. Since this is so little additional work, I recommend that you pretty up the wing.

2.2.2 Tail

I built models with horizontal stabilizers that were 20% and 25% of the area of the wing. This percentage includes the area of the elevator. Both worked fine, so I settled on 20%. The vertical stabilizer with the rudder is half that size or 10%.

The actual dimensions of the tail were arrived at empirically. 10 x 4 inches are nice round numbers and they gave me the area I needed.

I don't like elevator designs that are split into left and right halves with a joiner so the rudder can sit in between. Seems to me like an added complication. I chose to have the rudder sit above the elevator with a beveled cut on the rudder so it can clear the elevator when it moves up.

Since foamboard foam was my building material, using a single thickness sheet was a natural choice. In all my testing and crashes, I never had a tail break on me.

2.2.3 Fuselage

I settled on a fuselage that was about 80% as long as the wing. With a 30 inch (76 cm) wing, this works out to 24 inches (61 cm). It looks right and it gave me plenty of stability with a 20% sized tail.

My first prototype had no protection for the motor and a gentle nose down landing bent the motor shaft. My motor is about an inch squared (6.5 sq cm). Most of my prototypes had fuselages that were two inches high (5 cm) with the motor mounted near its top edge. This worked extremely well to protect the motor. After the stability, controllability, and crash resistance improved, I decided that 1.5 inches (3.8 cm) was plenty.

Coming up with a fuselage design that was light while being strong and stiff was very hard. The primary goal of most of my prototypes was to try out a new fuselage design. Most were dismal failures. I started relying heavily on strapping tape, which on hindsight wasn't good.

The very first prototype I built was a 1/3 scale paper airplane (see Figure 2.2 on the following page). I still have it, and it's significant because it had a triangular fuselage. I learned early on that sanding at an arbitrary angle

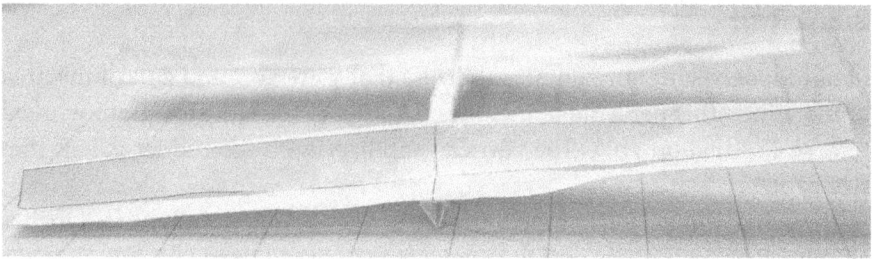

Figure 2.2 Paper Airplane
Note the triangular fuselage. This was a tandem wing design idea I was trying out. Future book subject?

without a jig is very hard to do. Not knowing how to make this shape work, I put it aside for a long time.

Then it occurred to me that using small dowels at the joints did away with the need for sanding. This was a major breakthrough. The fuselage design described in this book is both the strongest and lightest version I've built. Compared to my first prototype, crash survivability went from F to A+. This fuselage is incredibly stiff, having a small amount of flex only when twisted (not a major issue).

Most of my fuselages tapered in height towards the tail. This causes complications with the triangular shape. Since this design is so light anyway, I maintain a constant width and height from front to back.

Once I had a triangular fuselage, moving the tail servos to sit on top of it made a lot of sense. A very clean installation and it helps keep them from getting damaged in a bad landing.

2.2.4 Control Surfaces

The elevator and rudder are both about 40% of the width of the tail surfaces. This is to maximize their effectiveness.

Since ailerons are attached to the wings, a common goal is to maximize their efficiency. With this goal in mind, they are about 25% of the chord size.

Interestingly, in both of these cases the needed width works out to the same value. All control surfaces are 1.5 inches (3.8 cm) wide.

The simplest, least expensive, and most reliable control rods are solid piano wires with z bends at their ends. The problem is that making these z bends at exactly the right spot is pretty much impossible to do consistently. My clean solution is to bend the rods first and *then* use double sided tape to mount the servos where needed to make the length come out right.

2.2.5 Motor Mount

My earlier motor mounts were made using light aircraft plywood. This is great stuff, very strong and easy to work with. The main problem is that it's too thick to cut with a knife and too big to use a small saw. I was using a hand rotary tool and a drill press to shape them. As usual, I asked myself if there was a better way.

Craft sticks are incredibly inexpensive. They are easy to cut with a small hobby saw and work just fine as a motor mount.

Gluing on a misaligned motor mount leads to a poorly flying model. I decided that the best design was a simple motor mount with no downthrust that was very easy to build correctly. Adding washers to the motor screws solved the downthrust problem without complicating the design.

2.3 Power System

For a sport electric airplane, 10% of the total airplane weight should be the motor and 15% should be the battery. This is valid as long as you use a brushless motor, LiPo batteries, and fly for six minutes. I call this *Carlos' Power Rule*.

The actual flying weight of the model is about 7.5 ounces (213 grams). My power rule says that the motor should weigh 0.75 ounces (21 grams) and the battery should weigh 1.125 ounces (32 grams). I tried a few different electric motors and really liked the famous Blue Wonder. Great efficiency, durability, and value.

Description
ZIPPY Flightmax 500 mAh 2S1P 20C battery pack
Turnigy Plush 10A speed control
Turnigy 2730 1700Kv brushless outrunner motor
Slow Flyer 8 x 3.8 propeller

Table 2.2 Power System Components

Then I learned that they've recently released an improved version. Using better materials and construction, the manufacturer claims a 5% performance improvement over the Blue Wonder. This is only about a 2% increase in overall power system efficiency, but it's still something. New and improved products are constantly being released—check key vendor websites periodically.

I settled on a 500 mAh 2S battery with a maximum discharge rate of 20C or 10 amps. Weight is 1.3 ounces (36 grams). I can fly for about 15 minutes with this battery, which means that the discharge rate is about 2 amps (0.5 * 60/15).

Since I was going to be using four servos, I wanted to make sure that the BEC (battery eliminator circuit) in the speed control could handle them. That dictated that I use a two cell battery pack as opposed to three. It is easier for the speed control BEC to step down the voltage from a two cell pack. To compensate for the lower system voltage, I used a variant of the motor with a higher Kv (voltage constant).

The manufacturer's recommended propeller is a slow flyer 8 x 3.8 prop. That completed the power system (see Table 2.2).

Some quick calculations confirm the validity of these numbers. The flying speed about doubles at full throttle. The motor is good for 8 amps at full power, so that makes sense. A well-known rule in aviation is that quadrupling the power doubles the airspeed.

A handheld tachometer showed that the RPM at maximum throttle was

7,700 and at cruise it was 3,800. Thrust from a propeller increases as the square of the RPM, so this said that the cruise thrust was 24% of that available at maximum power. That sounded about right, too.

From watching the models fly, I've estimated that the cruising speed is about 10 mph (16 km/h), the maximum speed is 20 mph (32 km/h), and the stalling speed is less than 5 mph (8 km/h).

How do I know that these are the actual flying speeds? The last thing I do before I head for the flying field is get the current weather forecast. I know what the wind and gust speeds will be at the field before I get there. When the wind is about 10 mph, the model easily hovers at cruise speed. Once I flew with gusts of 20 mph and I was able to stay in one place without getting blown away. The stalling speed is similar to the cruise speed of my Vapor, which is about 5 mph.

2.3.1 RCadvisor's Calculator

I used my online power system calculator[1] to confirm the power system choices. It would take too much space to describe in detail everything that I did, but here are some highlights.

A year ago I conducted some power system studies to find a good small motor. It is critically important to compare motors by simulating the actual flying conditions and not by using theoretical performance numbers. My calculator makes this type of comparison very easy. This investigation is what led me to the Blue Wonder initially.

I used the calculator's optimizer to find the best propeller for my power system and airplane combination. I was primarily interested in maximizing the power duration while cruising, but I also wanted to make sure the efficiency at higher power settings was good, too.

Let's look at the data for my model in the calculator (see Figure 2.3 on the following page). The cruise speed and battery duration match my flight testing. Good! By looking at the chart (not shown), we can also see that the power system efficiency is near its peak at our cruise speed.

---

[1] www.RCadvisor.com

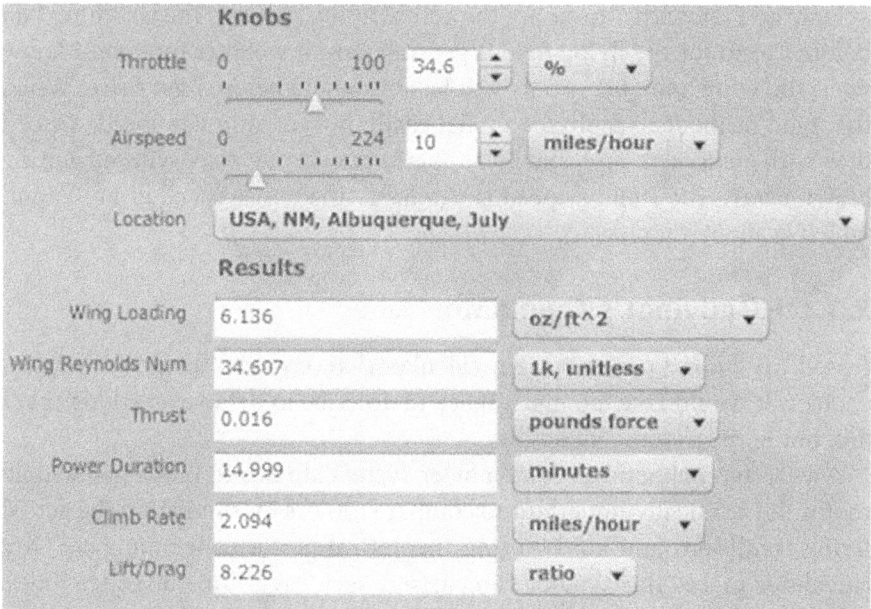

Figure 2.3 Airplane at Cruise
Closeup of the Knobs and Results panels of the airplane editor of RCadvisor's calculator.

I live in Albuquerque, New Mexico. That puts me about a mile up in altitude. The air density here is about 15% lower than it would be in another city near sea level. At the same airspeed, the wing and propeller produce less lift and drag at this altitude. The net effect is that the airplane needs to fly a little faster and the propeller needs to turn a little faster to fly the model. There is a difference, but don't lose sleep over it. Note that an electric motor is not affected by changes in air density.

The Reynolds number at cruise is only about 35,000. This is scary low. Analysis programs such as XFoil and my calculator have trouble making accurate predictions under these conditions. That is why some of the lines in the charts are very curvy.

How do I know that this throttle setting provides enough power to fly the airplane at the given airspeed? The key is to look at the climb rate in the results section. If it's positive, that means that there is an excess of power at that airspeed.

Looking at the power system while we are cruising around (see Figure 2.4 on the next page) reveals some interesting information. We are using 14 watts of power at this airspeed. The maximum power from the motor is about 57 watts (2 batteries * 3.6 volts * 8 amps). This is another check of our calculations: 4 * 14 watts = about 57 watts.

A 25 watt motor is probably powerful enough to fly this airplane. For indoor flying, since weight is so critical for the slow speeds required, a 10 gram motor with a 350 mAh 2S1P battery pack would be a great choice.

Note that our power system efficiency at cruise is only about 25%. The main problem is the propeller, which is only 45% efficient (you can see this by looking at the propeller editor, not shown here). The power system optimizer confirmed that this is the best that I can hope for.

When it comes to selecting a propeller, we are between a rock and a hard place. On the one hand, propeller efficiency is not very good at the low RPMs that we are turning. On the other hand, decreasing the diameter to bump up the RPMs will lower the overall efficiency. We could use a lower pitch to boost the efficiency at our RPMs, but then the high speed flight performance would suffer.

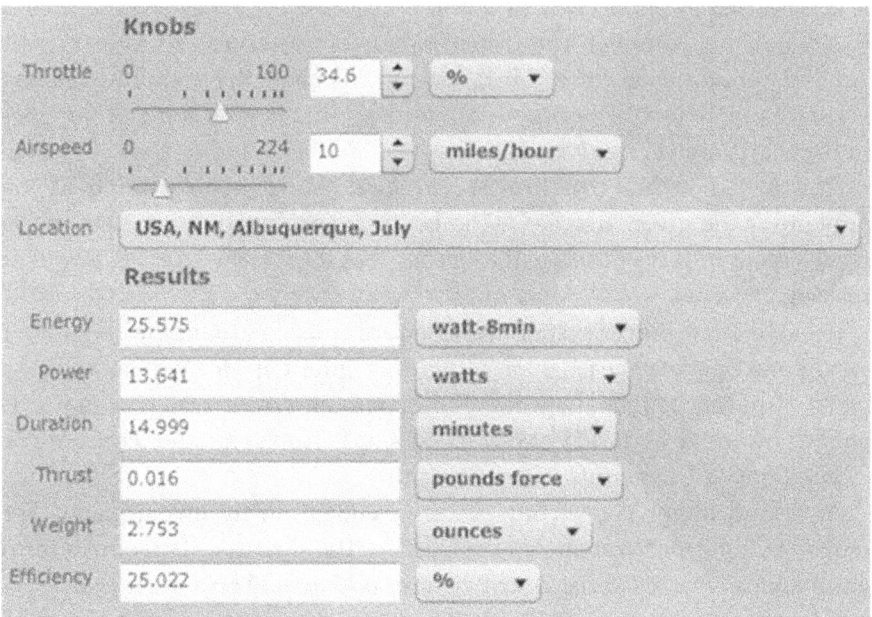

Figure 2.4 Power System at Cruise
Closeup of Power System editor.

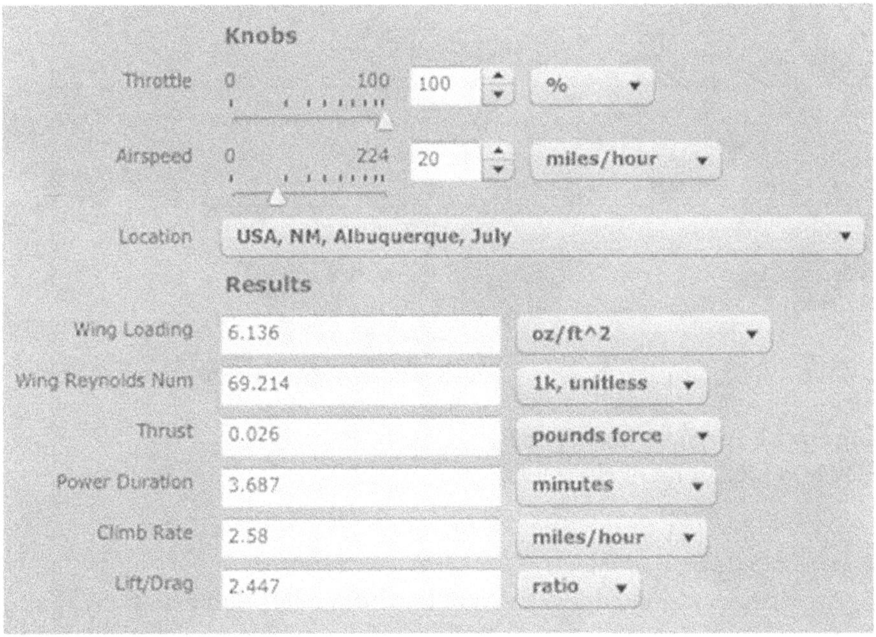

2 The Winner

Knobs		
Throttle	0 — 100 — 100	%
Airspeed	0 — 224 — 20	miles/hour
Location	USA, NM, Albuquerque, July	
Results		
Wing Loading	6.136	oz/ft^2
Wing Reynolds Num	69.214	1k, unitless
Thrust	0.026	pounds force
Power Duration	3.687	minutes
Climb Rate	2.58	miles/hour
Lift/Drag	2.447	ratio

Figure 2.5 Airplane at Maximum Speed
Closeup of airplane editor.

Bumping up the throttle to 100%, we match our expectation of 20 mph (see Figure 2.5). Note that at this speed we get less than four minutes of power. Since we are using energy at four times the rate of the cruise speed, that makes sense too (15 minutes/4).

By shutting the motor off, I got a quick check of the stalling speed (see Figure 2.6 on the next page). That looks to be about 4.7 mph (7.5 km/h).

Besides getting good performance out of my power system, I wanted to make sure I wouldn't burn anything up in the process. At maximum power the load on the motor is almost 8 amps (see Figure 2.7 on page 57). With a 20C rating on the battery, I knew that it was good for 10 amps. Ditto for the speed control. With the excellent cooling on the motor, I didn't expect that

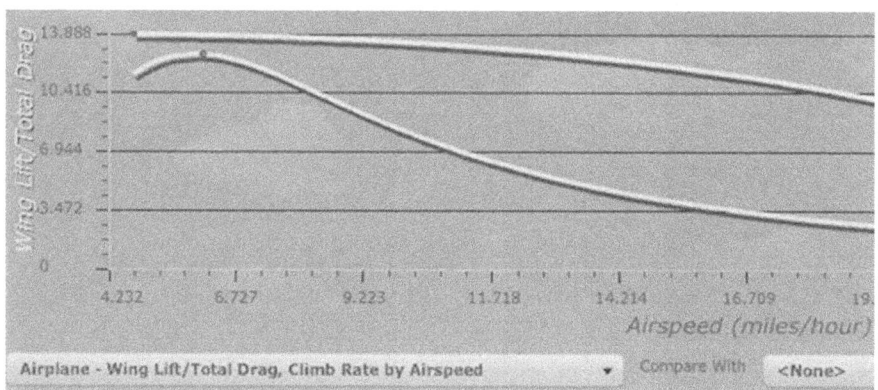

Figure 2.6 Airplane Stall Speed Power off. Closeup of chart.

8 amps would be a problem.

Are the motor and battery overkill for this model? Some may say that. I disagree. It is very nice to have the extra power when I need it, like when a gust comes out of nowhere. A 15 minute flight gives me plenty of time to relax and enjoy the model.

2.3.2 Field Testing Tools

I have some other tools that come in handy for taking measurements of the model. I don't feel that any of these are required, but they do help to understand what is going on.

A voltmeter belongs in every well-equipped workshop and field box. I'm always measuring battery voltages.

I've had a tachometer for a long time. It's very easy to measure the RPM of a motor, just don't try to do it indoors under a fluorescent light.

A wind speed meter (anemometer) is a recent acquisition. I heard a rumor that once two of these measured exactly the same wind speed. I've never

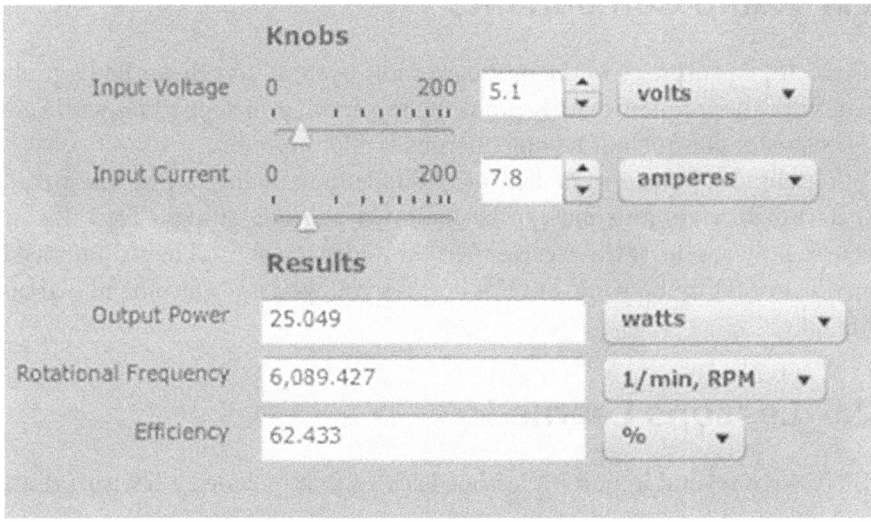

Figure 2.7 Motor at Maximum Power
These are the knobs and results from the motor editor. Power system throttle at 100%. Input Knobs reflect the values currently being used by the power system. Very handy!

seen it. In other words, don't expect great accuracy. But it will certainly be more than enough to get a feel for the flying speed of the model.

I have an Eagle Tree on-board logger that should be getting used more. Since my model is so light, I'm afraid that it might affect the flying qualities and duration a little too much.

2.4 Radio Components

There are no surprises in the on-board radio system. I've never had a problem with the torque from a 5 gram micro servo. It flies just fine with rudder-elevator control, but having ailerons is a lot more fun.

A great idea I had was to drill a small hole in the wing so that the spread spectrum receiver antenna can be mounted pointing straight up. This of course only applies if the receiver is right under the wing. I haven't noticed any loss of lift in the wing, but if it bothers you, you are welcome to seal up the hole.

2.5 Lessons Learned

There were several important lessons learned that included a few surprises!

Inventing a good completely original model airplane design is hard work.

There are just too many choices and blind alleys. Almost anything will fly, but a good and memorable design is hard to create. A look at the vast quantity of free designs available online easily confirms this.

There are few good test pilots around.

There are a lot more good pilots than good test pilots. Most people do not maiden model airplanes often enough to get good at diagnosing their problems, especially if they are severe.

A common mistake that would-be test pilots make is to assume they know what your ultimate goals are. It's human nature to assume that you are designing a model for a pilot just like them. You have to question their feedback to uncover hidden assumptions like these.

You don't want a test pilot guessing what the fix for a problem should be. You just want the unadulterated facts on what they observed.

Angles are hard to build accurately

Cutting or sanding at a specific angle is something I've never been able to do well. Most of the time building a jig is more trouble than it's worth. Cutting complex shapes is not far behind in degree of difficulty. I managed to avoid both of these trouble spots in my design.

It's much harder to build a stiff airplane than a strong airplane.

It's usually harder to get enough stiffness. Materials usually bend before they break. This bending can play havoc with the flying characteristics, even if the airplane does not break on you.

XPS foam is about four times stiffer, by weight, than common woods. I was very surprised when I discovered this. The problem is that it is so light that you need a lot of foam to make a part stiff enough for a component such as a fuselage.

A hardwood skeleton with a foam frame works really well.

This is a great combination. It's really inexpensive and the foam cushions the wood when you crash. It behaves like a composite structure this way. The models come together very fast.

2.6 Specifications

	U.S. Customary	Metric
Wing span	30 in	76.2 cm
Wing area	176 in²	1,135 cm²
Fuselage length	24 in	61 cm
Flying weight	7.5 oz	212.6 g
Maximum speed	20 mph	32 km/h
Cruise speed	10 mph	16 km/h
Stall speed	5 mph	8 km/h
Duration at cruise	15 min	15 min

Table 2.3 Summary Specs

	U.S. Customary	Metric
Span	30 in	76.2 cm
Chord	6 in	15.25 cm
Area	176 in²	1,135 cm²
Aspect ratio	5.1	5.1
Taper ratio	1	1
Thickness	5.8%	5.8%
Airfoil	KFm1	KFm1
Aileron width	1.5 in	3.8 cm
Aileron length	12 in	30.5 cm
Aileron to centerline	0.75 in	2 cm
Washout	0°	0°
Dihedral	0°	0°
Rearmost CG	40%	40%
Rearmost CG	2.4 in	6 cm

Table 2.4 Wing Specs

	U.S. Customary	Metric
Length	24 in	61 cm
Width	1.35 in	3.4 cm
Height	1.69 in	4.3 cm
Percentage of wingspan	80%	80%
Wing leading edge to nose	5 in	12.5 cm
Horiz stab leading edge to nose	21.5 in	55 cm

Table 2.5 Fuselage Specs

	U.S. Customary	Metric
Span	10 in	25.4 cm
Width	4 in	10.1 cm
Area	38 in^2	245 cm^2
Aspect ratio	2.6	2.6
Percentage of wing	21.6%	21.6%
Elevator width	1.5 in	3.8 cm
Elevator percentage	37.5%	37.5%

Table 2.6 Horizontal Stabilizer Specs

	U.S. Customary	Metric
Height	5 in	12.7 cm
Width	4 in	10.1 cm
Area	19 in^2	122.5 cm^2
Percentage of wing	10.8%	10.8%
Rudder width	1.5 in	3.8 cm
Rudder percentage	37.5%	37.5%

Table 2.7 Vertical Stabilizer Specs

3 Prepare to Build

You will need a few materials (see Table 3.1 on the next page) and tools to build this model.

3.1 Materials

All the materials except for the piano wire can be purchased at Wally World (also known as Walmart), though I much prefer the foamboard from Dollar Tree.

3.1.1 Foamboard

You will need one standard-sized sheet of foamboard to build the model. These measure 20 x 30 inches and are about 1/4 inch thick. Any brand and color of foamboard will work.

However, there is one brand of foamboard that I like above all others. Dollar Tree foamboard is an amazing product. Very inexpensive (just a dollar!), the paper glued to the foam comes off easily. I use rubbing alcohol and a large yard trash bag. Yes, the smell from the evaporating alcohol might be objectionable. Wet the foamboard on both sides with the alcohol, stick it in the bag, close it all up, and wait at least half an hour. The paper will just peel off, leaving behind a beautiful sheet of extruded polystyrene (XPS) foam. This sheet will be about 0.175 inch thick (4.5 mm).

My local Dollar Tree stores have the foamboard in stock only about half the time I walk in. When they have it, it's sitting on the aisle floor in a big box. You can special order an entire box of foamboard from them at no extra charge. It's 50 sheets and it'll cost you $50.

Material	Recommendation
Foamboard	standard-sized sheet from Dollar Tree
Dowels (x5)	1/8 inch from craft store
Laminating glue	Elmer's Extra Strength glue stick
Structural glue	Liquid Nails Small Projects
Craft sticks	regular size
Hinge tape	3M Nexcare Durable Cloth tape
Double-sided tape	Scotch Permanent Double Sided tape
Nylon tie	7 inch black
Piano wire	36 x 0.036 inch from hobby store
Hook and loop fastener	Velcro from craft store
Masking tape	inch-wide clean release painter's tape
Wax paper	supermarket

Table 3.1 Required Supplies

3.1.2 Dowels

Get the dowels from whomever has the lowest price. I go through the stack at the store and pick the straightest pieces. This is probably overkill on my part.

I see spruce as an unnecessary luxury in most cases. A clean piece of hardwood will have a comparable strength to weight ratio and cost much less.

Dowels are not always the size that they claim to be (see Table 3.2 on the facing page). The 1/8 inch dowels from Walmart and Michael's are a great match for the foam. These are generally the ones that I have used.

Problem is, the Walmart dowel is about 50% heavier and about 75% stronger than a standard sized 1/8 inch dowel. Will this cause you problems if you use a different brand that is smaller in size?

The dowels on the fuselage are there to stiffen the structure and to provide convenient gluing surfaces. The fuselage is very strong as it is. Using smaller

Dowel	Actual Size	Error
Hobby Lobby crafts 1/8	0.130 - 0.160	4% - 28%
Walmart and Michael's (Forster) 1/8	0.148	18%
JoAnn (Craftwood) 1/8	0.125	0%
Lowe's (Madison) 1/8	0.129	3%
Home Depot 1/8	0.125	0%
Walmart and Michael's (Forster) 3/16	0.183	-2%
Lowe's (Madison) 3/16	0.187	0%

Table 3.2 Actual Dowel Sizes
(1/8 = 0.125, 3/16 = 0.1875)

dowels than what I used will not cause a problem.

The wing leading edge dowel is there mostly to provide crash resistance and to help stiffen the wing. It's size is not critical, either.

The main spar dowel is there strictly to stiffen the wing. Remember that I never had a wing break on me when I built them without dowels. A smaller dowel here will probably be okay. But if you are using standard sized 1/8 inch dowels for the rest of the structure, I'd say that a 3/16 inch dowel would be a good idea here. This dowel size will stick out the bottom of the wing a small amount, but the structural adhesive should have no trouble bridging the gap between the foam surfaces.

The dowels from hardware stores like Lowe's and Home Depot are actually 48 inches long (122 cm), a full foot longer than what you find at craft stores. Buy two, cut them in half, and you have the fuselage supports.

3.1.3 Piano Wire

Piano wire is also called music wire. If you cannot find the exact size listed, just use the next largest size.

Hardware stores carry piano wire, but it's too thick for my needs. The only reliable local source I've found is hobby stores. I only use it for the control rods and there are many other ways to build those. It also comes in handy for landing gears, but I fly from grass fields where handlaunching is definitely the way to go.

I'm not a fan of E-Z connectors. I've had them come loose on me and I've read too many reports from others of similar problems. Properly used, I'm sure they work fine. But it's too easy to put them on wrong. There is nothing more reliable than a z bend on a single piece of piano wire.

I've never used z bend pliers, but they might make it easier to get the bends just right. You might find it helpful to attach a piece of masking tape to mark the spot where the bend needs to go.

3.1.4 Control Horns

Commercial control horns are inexpensive. I used them in the early prototypes. Then I asked myself if I could do better. I could.

Nylon ties work great as control horns. Mine are about seven inches long. The size is not critical. I cut them into 3/4 inch long pieces with one end angled at 45°. I drill a hole for the piano wire at the square end and they are ready to go (see Figure 4.15 on page 92).

I do have one warning. Nylon has just about the worst degradation under sunlight of any common material. If left outside in the sun, it will completely decay within one month. Manufacturers mix in carbon powder to dramatically improve its weathering properties. Moral: only use black nylon ties for control horns.

3.1.5 Hinge Tape

For a model this size, almost anything will work as a hinge tape. I prefer to seal my hinges. Makes for better efficiency.

I have nothing against Blenderm except it's price. I can get a much better value for comparable performance. The Nexcare Durable Cloth Tape is available at Walmart and other pharmacies. At hospital supply stores, it's called 3M Durapore Surgical Tape.

To separate the control surfaces, I slice across the foam at a 45° angle and flip one piece over. This results in a V shape that gives great freedom of movement. Sounds tricky, but I've never messed one up. I run the hinge tape on both sides, which is why I end up using so much of it on a single airplane.

3.1.6 Craft Sticks

These come in many different sizes. The size you use is not critical. The ones I use are 4 1/2 x 3/8 x 1/12.

3.1.7 Masking Tape

I use masking tape a lot to hold pieces. Mostly it's right after I apply glue. But I also use it to hold the control surfaces while I do the hinging and any other use that requires an extra hand.

Household masking tape will tend to have a weaker adhesive than painter's tape. For the delicate XPS foam surface, this is an advantage. Drafting tape has even lower adhesion than household masking tape, but may cost more.

A new type of painter's tape is less prone to damaging the foam surface and is labelled "clean release". The damage to the foam is purely a cosmetic surface blemish and it may not bother you.

3.2 Adhesives

3.2.1 Laminating Glue

Nothing beats a glue stick when it comes to gluing two large pieces of foam together face to face. It's ultra fast, easy, and holds great.

I've tested a lot of different glue sticks. Some are stronger than others, but they all pretty much work about the same. Something you definitely want to avoid are the clear or white glue sticks. Since it is going onto white foam, you'll never see whether you've applied enough or not. You want a glue stick that goes on blue or purple and then turns clear when it dries.

Since they dry very quickly, you want to work fast to avoid problems later. Don't worry about adding extra weight. Just spread plenty of glue on both sides and press the pieces firmly together. The piece can be handled almost right away, but I prefer to place weight on it and let it sit for at least half an hour.

3.2.2 Structural Glue

There are many glue choices for working with foam and wood. Like I said before, I don't like the polyurethane glues because of their foaming action. Epoxies are toxic, heavy, and hard to work with.

Another family of adhesives to avoid are the white aliphatic resin glues such as Weldbond or Aleene's Tacky Glue. They usually work fine. The problem is that they need lots of air and time to dry. Foam does not let the air go through. I've done tests with laminations and days later the glue was still wet. If you insist on using them, make sure you use the smallest amount that will do the job.

The cyanoacrylates (CAs) have their drawbacks, too. Foam-safe CA is expensive. I can never seem to get it to dry unless I use the CA accelerator, making it even more expensive. Joints can be brittle, not a good combination with flexible foam. Some have developed allergies to the fumes (less likely with the foam-safe variety).

I used to be a big fan of Liquid Nails Perfect Glue #1. In fact, this is the first glue that I came across that I really liked. Thick so it doesn't run, fast drying, easily sanded or trimmed after dry, and sticks great to foam and wood. I built most of my prototypes using it. There is only one little problem. It's just been discontinued!

A replacement adhesive, called Liquid Nails Small Projects, works just as well and is a lot less expensive. The primary active ingredient is polyvinyl acetate (PVA), which is the same as the common wood white glues. You can find it in the hardware section of Walmart and at other hardware stores. Use

3 Prepare to Build

just enough glue to bridge any gap between the two parts. Don't clamp the parts down. Apply just enough pressure to hold them steady. It'll be dry enough to manipulate after one hour.

Even if they appear to be dry, I like to let glues *and* tapes sit overnight before I put stress on them. It may surprise you to hear this, but the adhesives in tapes generally hold better after 24 hours have gone by since they were applied.

3.2.3 Glue Safety

Whatever adhesive you decide to use, avoid letting it touch your skin. Disposable cotton swabs (Q-tips) work almost as well as your fingers and are much safer. I've used disposable gloves in the past, but I generally find them cumbersome.

Manufacturers are required to prepare and make available Material Safety Data Sheets (MSDS) for glues. These can usually be found on their websites.

Glue sticks are very safe. There is no need to touch the glue once it has been applied, so I don't see any real problems here.

The structural adhesives are all used in small quantities, so follow the manufacturer's advice and avoid touching them directly, just in case.

3.3 Required Tools

3.3.1 Cutting and Drilling Tools

A hobby knife or single edge razor blade supply is essential. I start every project with a fresh #11 blade.

A small miter box and razor saw comes in handy for cutting the craft sticks and dowels.

A pin vise with a micro drill bit assortment is useful on most building projects.

If you use piano wire control rods, you'll need either z bend pliers or just regular needle nose pliers.

3.3.2 Sanding Tools

I have a sanding stick with medium and coarse permanent sandpaper that I'm always using. There's not a lot of sanding required, so that's really all you need.

3.3.3 Measuring and Marking Tools

I have two rulers that I'm using constantly. The first is one yard long and made out of metal. It has U.S. customary units on one side and metric units on the other. I mostly use it for guiding the blade when I'm cutting the foam.

The other is a 90° ruler with markings on both sides. I use it to measure and mark the foam. Being able to flip it over to measure from the other side is very handy.

You can use a soft pencil to mark the parts. My preferred marking tool is an Ultra Fine Retractable Sharpie permanent marker. I can grab it and use it with one hand, while the other holds down the ruler. It requires little force, so that the foam is not damaged. I wish the line it draws were a little thinner, but it's thin enough.

3.4 Optional Tools

I have a digital caliper that I'm using all the time. Works great with the piano wire, but I even use it to measure the dowels.

A digital scale accurate to one gram comes in handy.

A rotary tool and drill press can come in handy sometimes. If you don't already have these, don't bother getting them.

I have a digital angle gauge. I hardly ever use it, but when I do, it saves me a lot of head scratching.

A prop balancer is a recent acquisition. So far, using it has been a non-event. All the props I've tested were already perfectly balanced. But I expect it to pay for itself sooner or later.

3.5 Work Area

I have a cutting mat slightly larger than a piece of foamboard marked with one-inch squares. It's very handy to line up the foam to the squares before I cut to make sure the cut is straight.

4 Building

Time for the rubber to hit the road. This chapter describes in detail the steps for building the model. Important: read through the entire chapter before you start building.

The sequence given is not arbitrary, though some flexibility exists. For example, the vertical stabilizer, horizontal stabilizer, wing, and fuselage can be built in any order.

As described, the model uses an American standard-sized sheet of foamboard as it's core building material. This is 20 x 30 inches. Outside the United States, the closest size would be A1, which is 59.4 x 84.1 cm (23.4 x 33.1 inches). It is up to the reader to use a subset of an A1 sheet or to scale up the dimensions given in the specifications (see Section 2.6 on page 59).

For the sake of clarity and to avoid confusion, I have decided to only use units of inches in this chapter. All of the critical dimensions have already been provided using metric units in the specifications section.

4.1 Make Kit Parts

I like to mark the parts on the foamboard while the paper is still attached. Then I cut the parts out, remove the paper using alcohol or water, and the parts are ready to be used.

Cutting the dowels ahead of time also makes sense. This way you are making yourself a nice little airplane kit. While you are at it, you might want to make two!

Size (inches)	Description
30 x 6	main wing
30 x $2\frac{1}{4}$	wing step
$23\frac{7}{8}$ x $1\frac{1}{2}$ (x2)	fuselage sides
24 x 1	fuselage top
10 x 4	horizontal stabilizer and elevator
5 x 4	vertical stabilizer and rudder
$3\frac{5}{8}$ x $1\frac{1}{4}$	wing bottom support
1 x $1\frac{1}{2}$ triangles (x4)	internal fuselage reinforcements
$\frac{1}{2}$ x $2\frac{1}{2}$ (x2)	vertical stab reinforcements

Table 4.1 Foam Parts

Length (inches)	Description
24 (x3)	fuselage reinforcements
30	wing main spar
27	wing leading edge
$1\frac{5}{8}$ (x2)	motor mount supports

Table 4.2 Dowel Parts

4.1.1 Mark Foam Parts

Sometimes the foam has slightly crushed edges. Do what you can to avoid using these edges, but don't worry too much about it. Also, sometimes the edges are not quite square to each other. This is rarely a serious problem. Check the edges, and if they are not square, mark off a thin strip to cut off.

Lay out the foam parts in the order given (see Table 4.1 on the preceding page). If you do that, I promise you'll stay out of trouble. I usually put the wing on one side and the fuselage pieces on the opposite side. That way I have a little bit of elbow room in case the knife slips as I cut the foam pieces out.

I always mark all the lines before I cut them (see Figure 4.1 on the following page). It's a way of double checking my measurements. More importantly, then I can see right away if the ruler shifts while I'm cutting. This technique has saved me many times.

4.1.2 Cut Foam Parts

Grab a fresh blade before you cut the parts out. It is common for the blade to grab the foam a little bit as it cuts. Don't worry about it.

Lay out the ruler and cut the parts out. I make about three strokes with the blade before I'm completely through the part. I cut long pieces like the wing in two sections to avoid making very long blade strokes. The key is not letting the ruler slide as you press against it. It goes without saying that the blade should be at 90° to the cutting surface. It may help to practice first with a scrap piece of foamboard (see Figure 4.2 on page 77).

4.1.3 Remove Paper

The foamboard has paper glued to both sides of it. On the better brands, there are also thin layers of plastic. You need to remove all of this.

You might as well remove the paper from the entire sheet of foamboard, including the scrap pieces. They are no good to you with the paper on, anyway.

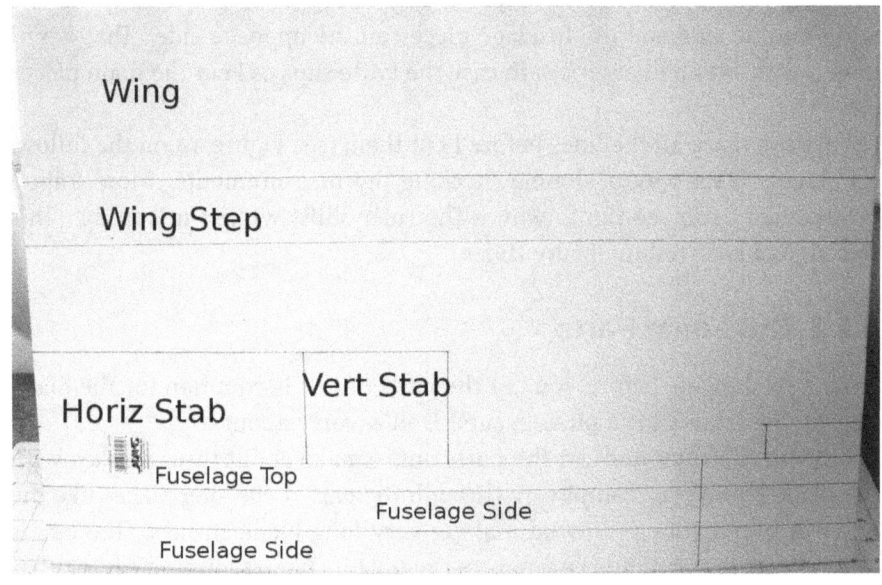

Figure 4.1 Mark Foam Parts
Wing pieces on top, tail pieces in the middle, and fuselage on bottom.

4 Building

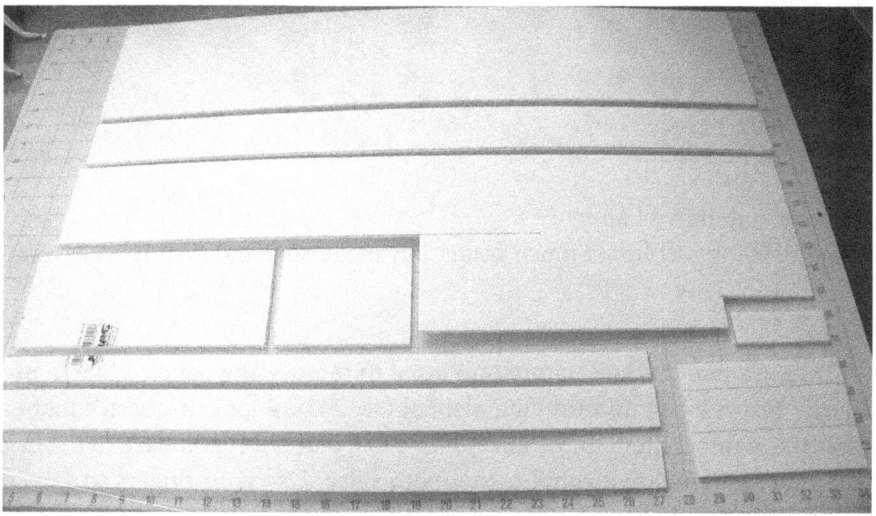

Figure 4.2 Cut Foam Parts
A fresh blade works wonders on the quality of the cuts.

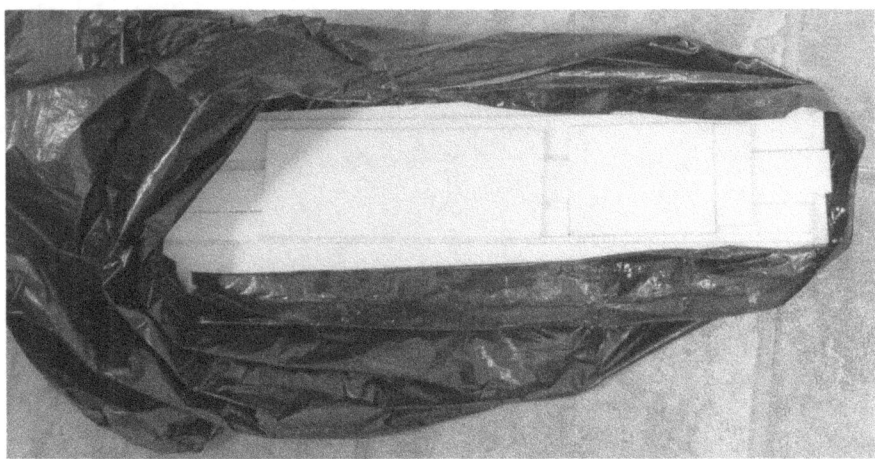

Figure 4.3 Remove Paper
Using rubbing alcohol is much faster, but make sure the area is well-ventilated.

There are two methods commonly used to remove the paper. I like to use a large garbage bag and rubbing alcohol (see Figure 4.3). It doesn't matter what the water content of the alcohol is. Put a piece of foamboard in the bag and pour just enough alcohol to wet both sides. Use your fingers to spread out the alcohol. The goal is not to soak the paper but to make sure it's wet. Yes, do this in a well-ventilated area. Add another piece of foamboard to the bag and repeat the process until all the pieces are inside. Close up the bag and let it sit for at least half an hour.

If you don't use the foamboard from Dollar Tree, the paper may be harder to remove. Leave it soaking in the alcohol for at least an hour. Using a pair of tweezers, pinch the edge of the corner of the foamboard. The idea is to just grab the paper (see Figure 4.4 on the next page). Once you start it coming off, you can use your fingers to continue pulling it loose. Other brands tend to use multiple layers, including a thin layer of plastic right next to the foam. Make sure you've got them all.

4 *Building* 79

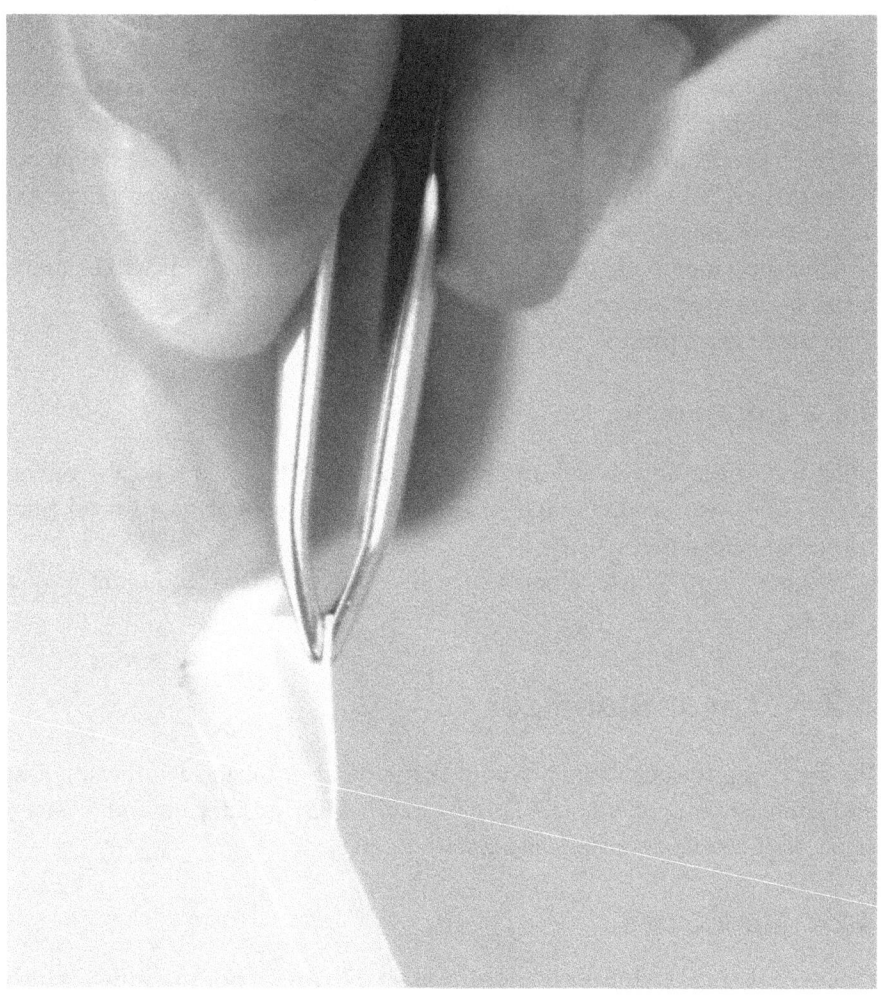

Figure 4.4 Using Tweezers to Remove Paper
Looking at the edge of the foamboard.

Sometimes the paper just refuses to come off. Make sure the entire surface, on both sides, is wet. Then put it back in the garbage bag and wait another half an hour.

The other method is to use a bath tub and water. This is even less expensive and you don't have to deal with the fumes from the evaporating alcohol. Close up the drain and put a few inches of water in the tub. Soak the pieces of foamboard. You'll need something to weigh them down. Wait overnight before removing the paper.

After the paper is all gone, you need to let the foam dry. This will be much faster if you used alcohol.

Now the foam pieces are ready to be used.

4.1.4 Cut Dowels

I like to cut the dowels before I start gluing (see Figure 4.5 on the facing page). The wing leading edge and motor mount supports will need final trimming before they are used.

You have now put together a nice little kit of parts (see Figure 4.6 on page 82).

4.2 Vertical Stabilizer

We are going to start assembly with the vertical stabilizer. It's the smallest and simplest component. It'll help us build skills for later on and is easily replaced if a serious mistake is made.

4.2.1 Mark Lines

Since the vertical stabilizer is almost square, be careful not to confuse which way it's supposed to go. The height is half that of the horizontal stabilizer, or five inches. The width of both is four inches.

Mark the line for the rudder $1\frac{1}{2}$ inches in on the longer side.

4 *Building* 81

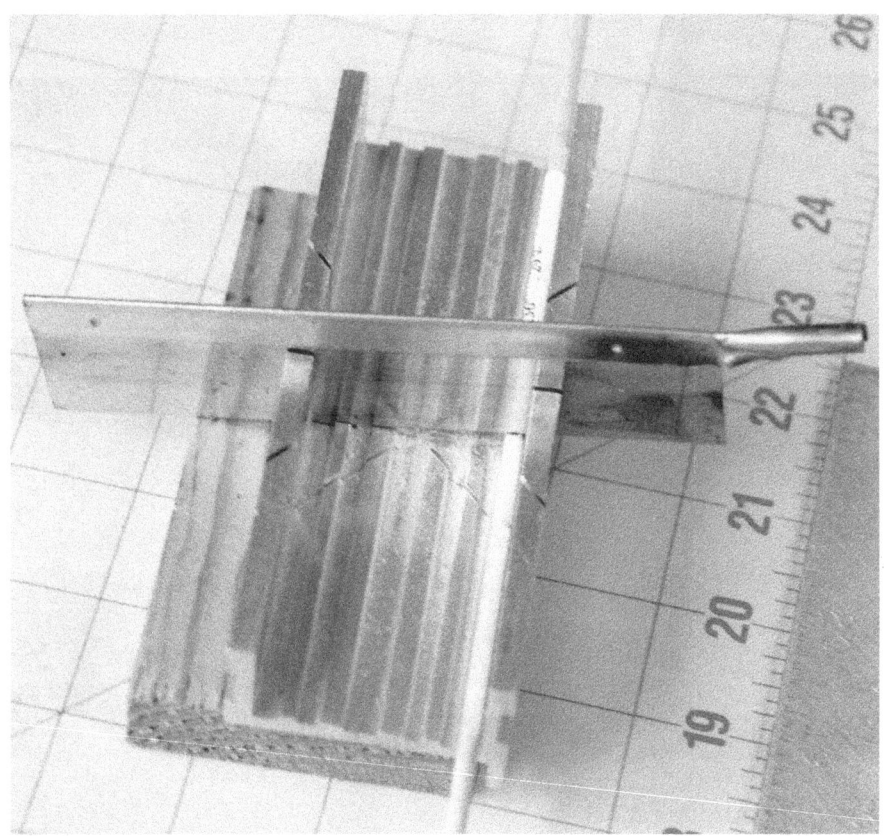

Figure 4.5 Cut Dowels
I like to use a razor saw and miter box.

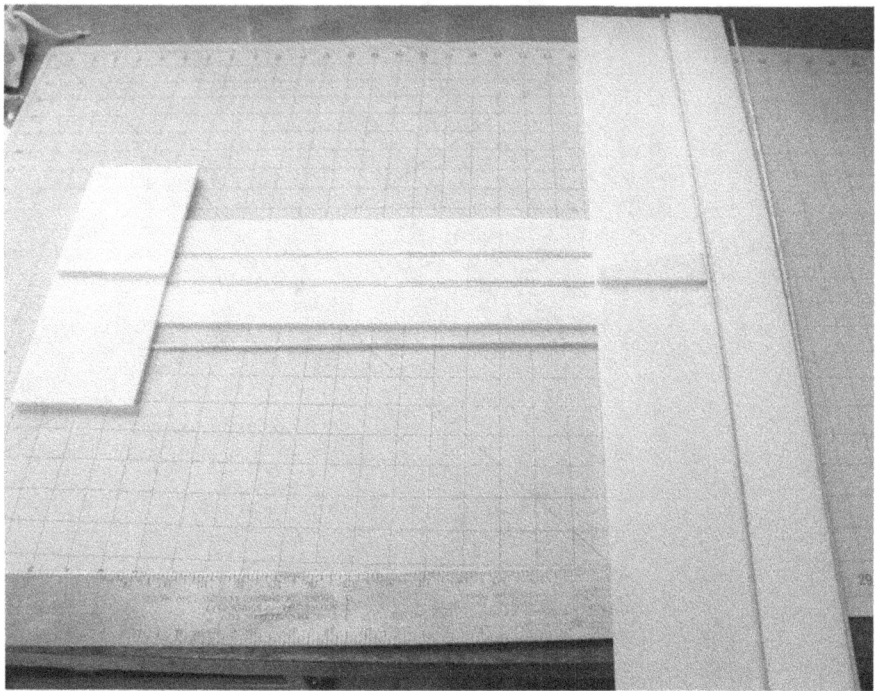

Figure 4.6 Airplane Mock-up
This is the general layout of the major airplane parts.

The airplane will fly better if all the corners of the flying surfaces are cut in a rounded shape and the forward-facing edges are sanded to smooth them out. Don't do these steps yet! All you are going to do now is to mark the circular shape on the corners.

You can draw the quarter circles freehand, but they'll look better if you use the bottom of a can or container as a pattern. If you have a compass handy, you might as well use it.

You'll be flipping the rudder over after you cut it. So mark two quarter circles on opposite corners (see Figure 4.7 on the following page).

You will need to cut a bevel on the rudder so it clears the elevator. 45° is a good angle to use. Since the rudder is upside down right now, mark it at its top.

4.2.2 Cut Hinge

All of the hinges have to be cut from the side *opposite* where the servo will be. For example, since the aileron servo is on top, you need to cut the ailerons from the bottom. Since the rudder servo horn is on the left side (as viewed from the rear of the airplane), you need to cut the rudder hinge from the right side (see Figure 4.8 on page 85).

The idea is to cut the control surface out at a 45° angle (see Figure 4.9 on page 86). The cut piece is then flipped over, yielding 90 degrees of motion in both directions. I only use one ruler on top to line up the blade. Some use two rulers to guide the blade, one on top and another below the piece to be cut. Feel free to use whatever method works for you. I've never had to throw out a piece because of a bad cut. But if you do throw one out, so what? Foam is cheap.

4.2.3 Cut Rudder Bevel

You need to cut a 45° bevel into the rudder so that the elevator can move up. Be careful to do this on the bottom of the rudder, not the top (see Figure 4.10 on page 87).

Figure 4.7 Mark V Stab Lines
Note how it is taller than wider.

4 Building

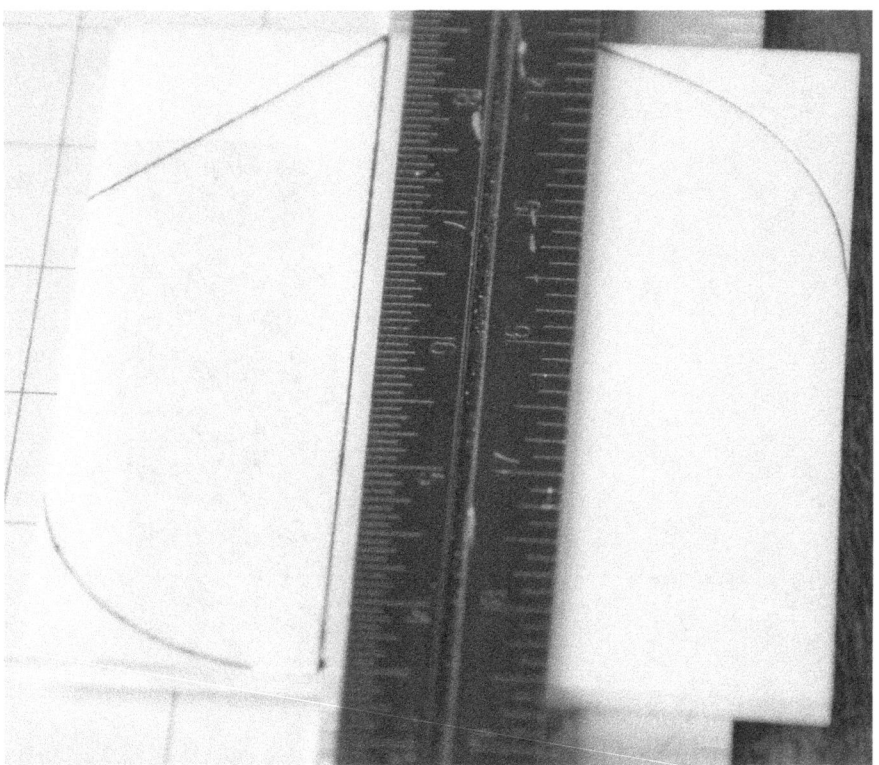

Figure 4.8 Prepare to Cut Rudder Hinge
We are going to cut from the right side of the vertical stabilizer. The rudder is upside down.

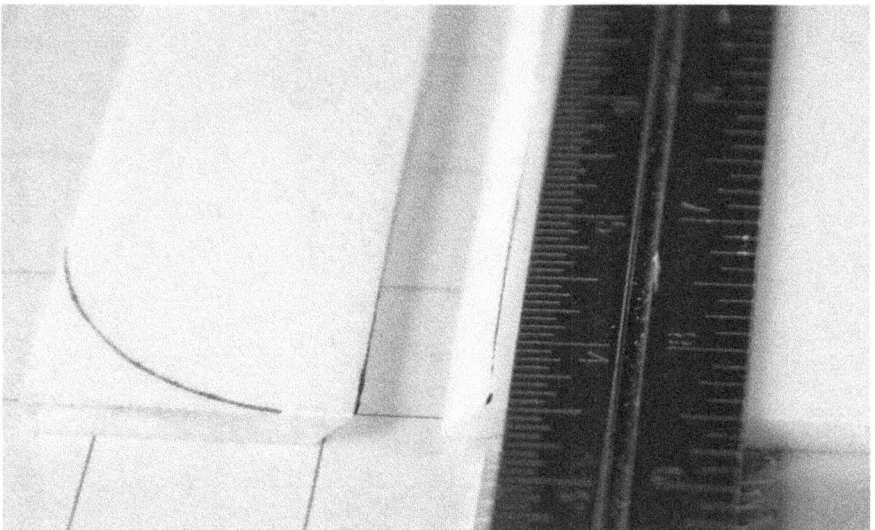

Figure 4.9 Cut Rudder Hinge
We cut at a 45° angle in one stroke.

4 *Building*   87

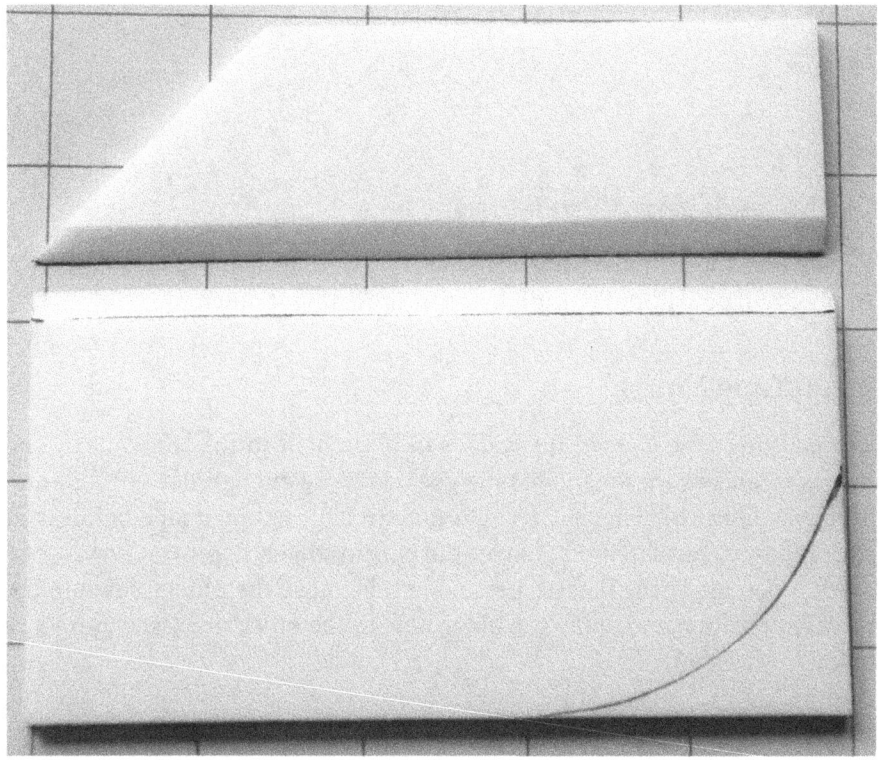

Figure 4.10 Cut Rudder Bevel
Cut it on the bottom of the rudder after it has been flipped over.

Figure 4.11 Tape Rudder Hinge Side 1
Apply the tape without tension by gently pressing it down.

4.2.4 Tape Hinge

Use masking tape to hold the rudder in place bent to the left at 180°. The idea is to make sure the hinge tape goes on loose enough not to cause any problems later (see Figure 4.11). Do not stretch the hinge tape before you stick it down. Just lay it down over the parts and gently press it down.

After you apply the hinge tape on one side, move the rudder down to the 90° right position and apply the hinge tape to the other side (see Figure 4.12 on the next page).

4.2.5 Cut Round Corners

I cut the corners freehand, following the curved lines previously drawn. The cut doesn't have to be perfect, since you are going to come back later and sand the curve smooth (see Figure 4.13 on page 90).

4 *Building*   89

Figure 4.12 Tape Rudder Hinge Side 2
The angle doesn't have to be a full 90°.

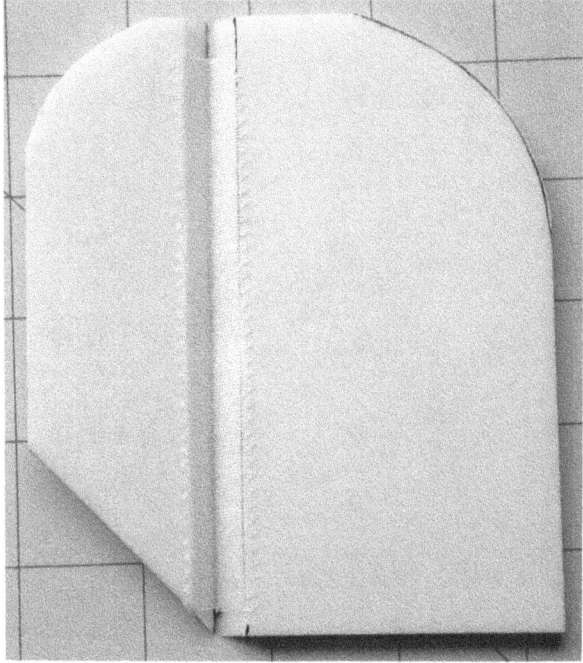

Figure 4.13 Round Vert Stab Corners
You'll be sanding these smooth later.

4 Building

Figure 4.14 Control Horns
Use the two closest in size for the ailerons.

4.2.6 Mount Control Horn

I make my control horns out of seven inch long black nylon ties. First I cut it into pieces $1\frac{1}{2}$ inches long. Then I cut those pieces in half at a 45° angle, creating two control horns. You need a total of four control horns for this model. Pick the two that are closest in size and use them for the ailerons (see Figure 4.14).

The piano wire used for the rudder, elevator, and ailerons is all the same size. Therefore you can drill the holes in the control horns all at the same time.

To make the holes, I use a drill bit the same size as the piano wire or slightly larger if I don't have one the same size. The fit will be snug, but that

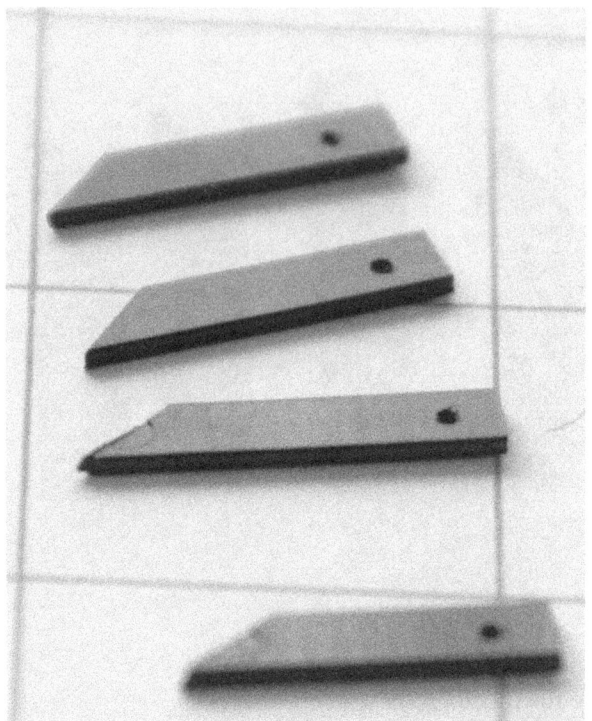

Figure 4.15 Control Horn Holes
Put the holes all in the same relative positions.

is what you want (see Figure 4.15).

Cutting the slot in the rudder for the control horn will be harder with a single edge razor blade than with a #11 blade. A good place to cut the slot is 3/4 inch up from the bottom of the rudder. Always mount the control horns at 90° to the hinge line (see Figure 4.16 on the next page).

Test fit the control horn first before you glue it in place. The goal is to have the hole right over the hinge line or right *behind* it, slightly over the rudder (see Figure 4.17 on the facing page).

4 Building   93

Figure 4.16 Control Horn Slot
Cut the slot at 90° to the hinge line.

Figure 4.17 Rudder Control Horn Side View
Always keep the hole to the right of the hinge line.

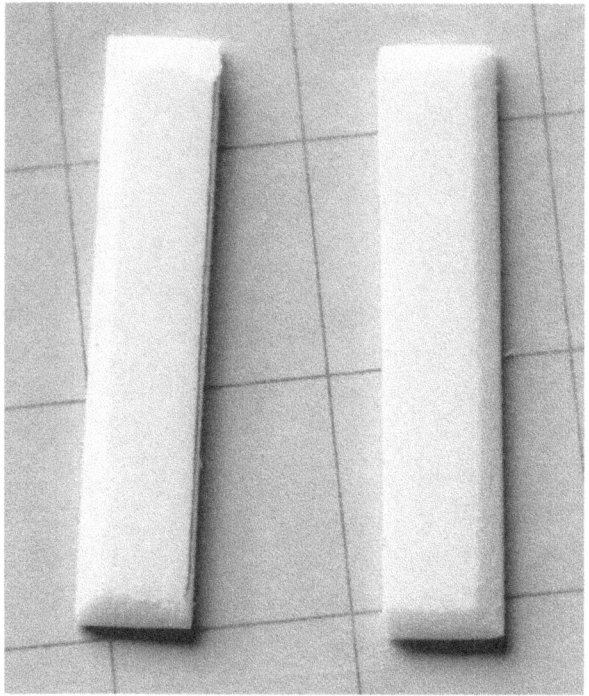

Figure 4.18 Vert Stab Side Supports
Round the supports on three sides.

Once you are happy with it, take some structural glue, fill up the slot with the glue, and fix the control horn in place.

4.2.7 Glue on Supports

Two small pieces of foam are used as vertical stabilizer supports (see Figure 4.18). For this one, you can either use the structural glue or the laminating glue stick. It's always easier to use a glue stick.

The key to the glue stick is to be generous and to move fast. Apply it to both surfaces and press the parts firmly together. Make sure the supports are clear of the rudder on the back. Stand up the vertical stabilizer on a piece of wax paper to make sure the supports are flush on the bottom (see Figure 4.19 on the following page).

4.2.8 Sand Edges

Gently sand the leading edge, rounded corners, and top of the vertical stabilizer. The idea is to remove all sharp corners and put a gently rounded shape on everything. It's probably better not to sand the rudder at all.

Now set it aside, since you won't be needing it for a little while.

4.3 Horizontal Stabilizer

Not surprisingly, this one is very similar to the vertical stabilizer which we just finished.

4.3.1 Mark Lines

Before you do anything else, take a look at the piece of foam. There's a good chance there'll be a slight curve on it along the long axis. Not critical, but orient it so that the ends of the curve are pointing up. Write a small letter B on it so that you know what the *bottom* side is.

Mark the line for the elevator $1\frac{1}{2}$ inches in on the longer side. Draw it on the bottom.

Mark the quarter circles on the four corners.

You need an extra set of lines, but don't extend them all the way back to the elevator. Don't worry about it if you do extend them by mistake (like I did in the pictures). Mark the centerline on both the top and the bottom. On the bottom, draw an extra set of lines $\frac{5}{8}$ of an inch away on both sides of the centerline. On the top, draw them $\frac{3}{8}$ inch away on either side. These lines will be used later to guide the mounting of the fuselage and vertical stabilizer, respectively (see Figure 4.20 on page 97).

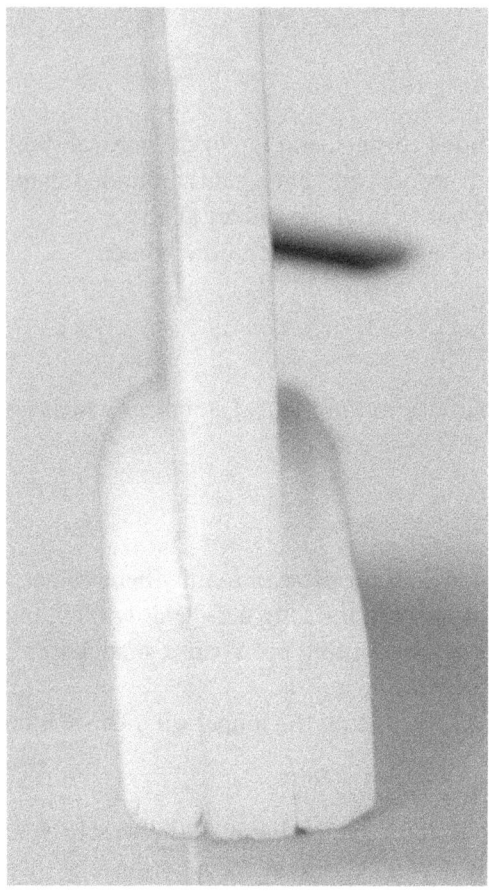

Figure 4.19 Vert Stab Side Supports Mounted
Stay clear of the rudder. Looking at the front of the vertical stabilizer. The bottom of the three pieces is flat.

Figure 4.20 Horiz Stab Marked Lines
My lines extended into the elevator, which is not necessary.

4.3.2 Cut Hinge

Since the elevator control horn will be on top, the hinge needs to be cut from the bottom. As before, cut it at a 45° angle (see Figure 4.21 on the following page).

4.3.3 Tape Hinge

Use masking tape to hold the elevator in place bent up at 180°. The idea is to make sure the hinge is loose enough not to cause any binding later.

After you apply the hinge tape on one side, flip the elevator over to the opposite 90° position and apply the hinge tape to the other side. As before, make sure not to stretch the tape before you press it down.

The hinge tape should extend from one end of the control surface to the other. It is not a problem if one or both sides are a little short.

Figure 4.21 Horiz Stab Hinge Cutting
This is how I cut my hinges. You need to keep your fingers well clear of the blade.

4 Building

Figure 4.22 Completed Horiz Stab
Viewed from the top. The ends of the hinge V point down. This one has the control horn. It's better to wait until final assembly to put it on.

4.3.4 Cut Round Corners

I cut the corners freehand, following the curved lines previously drawn. The cut doesn't have to be perfect, since you are going to sand the curve smooth.

4.3.5 Sand Edges

Gently sand the leading edge into a rounded shape, the rounded corners, and the sides of the horizontal stabilizer. It's probably better not to sand the elevator at all.

Another piece knocked off (see Figure 4.22). Congratulations, you are on a roll!

4.4 Wing

Given the skills we've learned so far, building the wing will be easy.

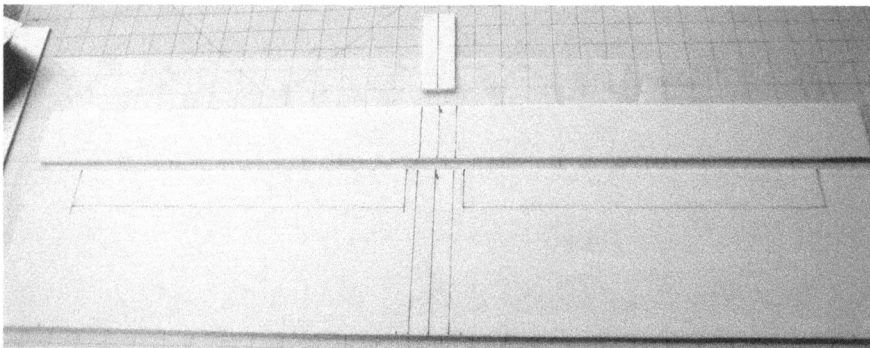

Figure 4.23 Marking Lines on Wing
Viewed from the bottom.

4.4.1 Mark Lines

Like the horizontal stabilizer, there will probably be a spanwise curve to the wing foam pieces. Position the wing and step so that this curve has the tips pointing upwards. Write a small letter B on the bottom of both of these pieces.

Mark the wing centerline on both the top and bottom of both wing pieces. Like we did with the horizontal stabilizer, mark lines $\frac{5}{8}$ of an inch away from the centerline on the bottom of both pieces.

Mark the locations of the ailerons on the bottom of the wing. These are 12 inches long and $1\frac{1}{2}$ inches wide. The inside edge of each aileron is one inch away from the centerline (see Figure 4.23).

Mark the quarter circles on the four corners. You will need a bigger circular template than you used for the tail. Make sure these circles don't touch the ailerons.

I like to draw a line on the bottom of the main wing piece marking the extent of the bottom step. Makes it easier to know how far to apply the laminating glue stick.

4.4.2 Cut Ailerons

The ailerons are nice and rectangular, so they are not too hard to cut. Don't forget to cut them at a 45° angle from the bottom.

To make sure I don't confuse them, I like to write the letters R and L on the hinge line of the right and left ailerons, respectively.

So that the ailerons don't touch the wing as they move up and down, cut $\frac{1}{16}$ inch from the end of each one.

When the ailerons are flipped over, they'll stick out the back of the wing a small amount. You can leave them like that, but for aesthetic reasons, I always trim them so that they match the wing trailing edge.

Invariably I cut a little too far and do some damage to the wing. From hard experience I've learned that these stray cuts are where breaks in the wing start. Fill them in with structural glue.

4.4.3 Tape Ailerons

Tape the ailerons exactly like you did the rudder and elevator.

There's an extra step here. Since the ailerons are so long, I've learned that they work better if they are reinforced. Apply hinge tape the full length of the ailerons on the bottom. If you have inch-wide strapping tape handy, you can use that here instead.

Look over the repaired foam at the aileron inside corners. As added protection, placing a strip of hinge tape across the cut area on the *top* side of the wing won't hurt (see Figure 4.24 on the next page). Do this after aileron hinging. Strapping tape works well for this, too.

4.4.4 Laminate Bottom Step

Working quickly, generously apply the glue stick to both pieces. Push the two pieces together firmly while making sure the edges are lined up. It is best to do this while the pieces are laying flat against your worktable. That way they'll also be flat after the glue dries (see Figure 4.25 on page 103).

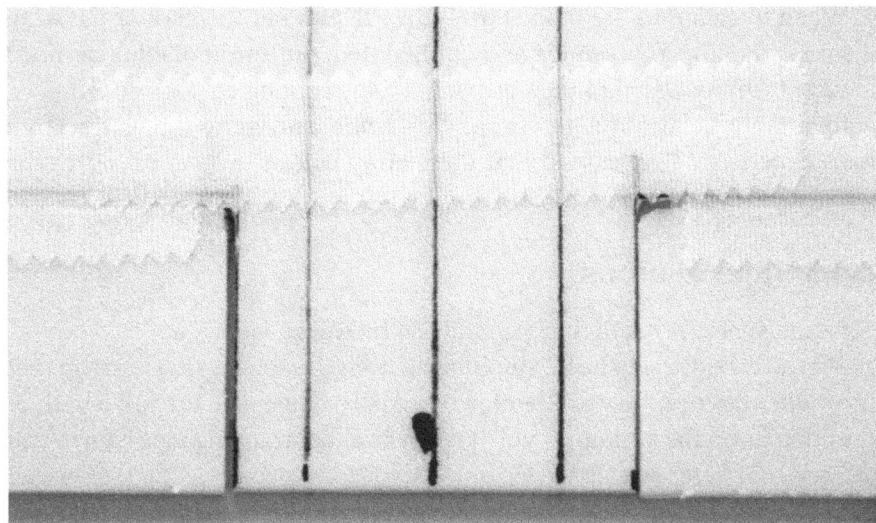

Figure 4.24 Wing Reinforcement Viewed from the top.

4 Building

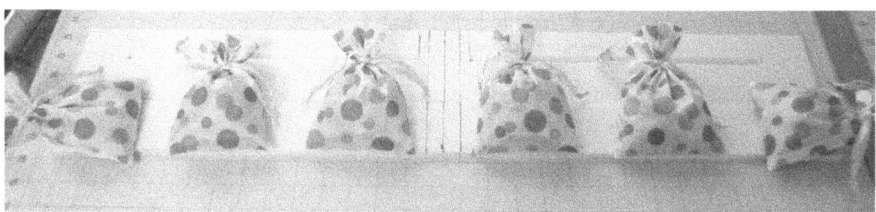

Figure 4.25 Wing Lamination
Weigh it down evenly.

I have a set of small cloth bags filled with small stones. They act like small sand bags. I like them because they don't mark the foam. The stones can be either those used in aquariums or in floral arrangements. The bags I got were for party favors. Some folks fill cotton socks and them sew them shut.

4.4.5 Glue Main Spar and Wing Support

Use the structural adhesive with the main spar. Use masking tape to hold in place.

Use the structural glue to attach the wing bottom support to the bottom of the wing (see Figure 4.26 on the next page).

4.4.6 Glue Leading Edge Spar

We need to use the structural glue on the wing leading edge spar. It's cut short to account for the rounded wing tips.

Flip the wing over so that it's rightside up. We want this spar to line up with the fuselage top spars later. That means that it needs to be glued to the *bottom* half of the leading edge, right in front of the wing. It actually increases the wing chord and wing area slightly. To keep it from sticking to your work table, use a piece of wax paper under the wing when you glue it on (see Figure 4.27 on page 105).

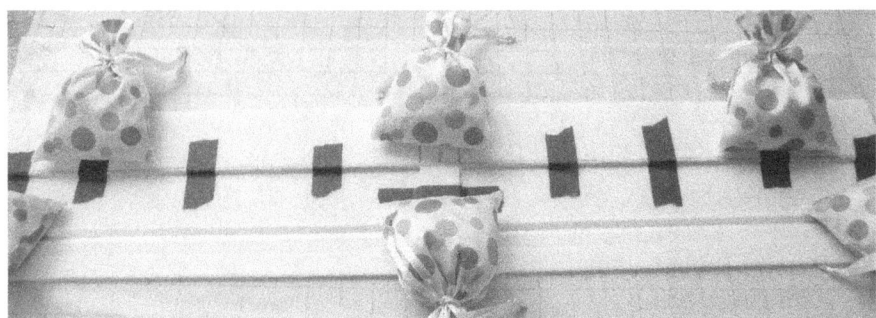

Figure 4.26 Wing Main Spar
Use the structural glue on the wing bottom support, too.

4.4.7 Cut Round Corners

As before, cut the corners off of the wing following the patterns previously drawn.

4.4.8 Sand the Edges

Now that the wing is almost done, we can finish it off by sanding it. As with the tail, do not sand the trailing edge.

We are done with the wing (see Figure 4.28 on page 106).

4.5 Fuselage

The fuselage is an interesting structure and I'm sure it'll be a little different from everything you've built before. Nevertheless, it's easy to put together.

4.5.1 Glue Dowels to Top Foam Piece

Glue the top two fuselage dowels to the sides of the fuselage top foam piece. Similar to the wing leading edge dowel, we need to make sure these dowels sit flush with the top side of the foam piece (which is upside down). The

4 *Building*

Figure 4.27 Wing Leading Edge
The wing is seen from the top. The leading edge dowel sits in front of the wing, glued to the bottom step. The masking tape is holding it down to the worktable.

Figure 4.28 Completed Wing
Looking at the bottom, with tape where the fuselage will go.

dowels are slightly smaller than the foam piece, so this is important to get right.

Apply the structural glue to the dowels and then use masking tape to hold them down while the glue dries. As before, put the assembly over a piece of wax paper (see Figure 4.29 on the facing page).

4.5.2 Add the Triangular Supports

I recommend that you use four of these, but you can use more if you want (see Figure 4.30 on page 108). At a minimum, use one at the front of the fuselage, at the back of the fuselage, and at the position of the wing leading and trailing edges. Add more between these positions as desired.

Test fit the fuselage side foam pieces and make sure the triangles are all the same size and fit well. Use the structural glue to glue the triangles to the top fuselage foam piece (see Figure 4.31 on page 108).

4.5.3 Affix Motor Mount Supports

Glue the motor mount side supports to the sides of the front foam triangle. Make sure the bottom ends of these dowels can accommodate the fuselage bottom dowel in the next step (see Figure 4.32 on page 109).

4 Building

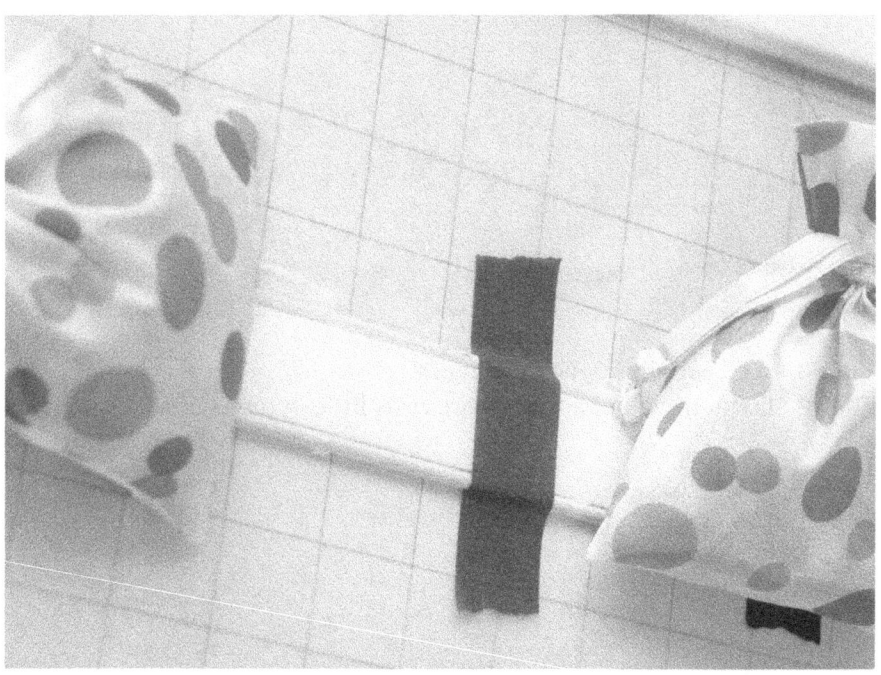

Figure 4.29 Fuselage Top
Glue the dowels on both sides.

Figure 4.30 Fuselage Support Triangles
Four is all you need, but adding more costs little in terms of added weight.

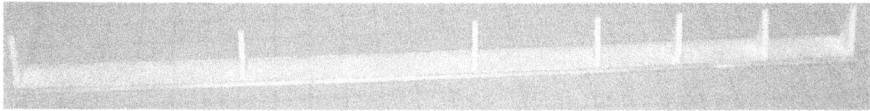

Figure 4.31 Fuselage Support Triangles Glued On
Glue them to the top of the fuselage first.

4 *Building*

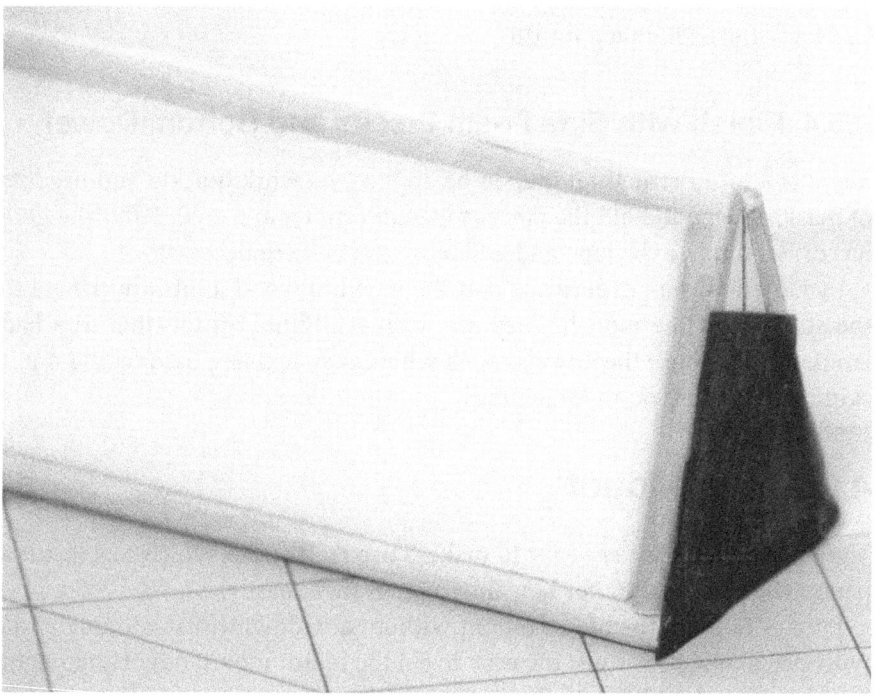

Figure 4.32 Fuselage Nose
Completed fuselage nose detail with masking tape. Bottom dowel is at the top of the picture.

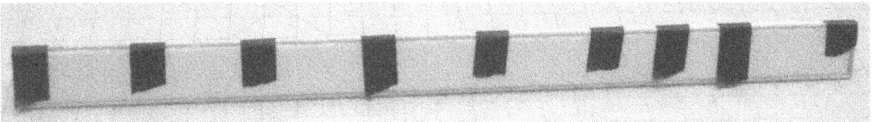

Figure 4.33 Fuselage Sides
Use lots of masking tape for this step.

4.5.4 Finish with Side Foam Pieces and Bottom Dowel

There is a lot of structural glue to be applied, so work quickly and use lots of masking tape to hold the pieces together (see Figure 4.33). After the glue has dried, remove the tape and add more glue where necessary.

I've learned from experience that the wood to wood joints are critical to the strength of the model. They are what really hold it together in a bad landing. Make sure the dowels touch where they are supposed to and don't skimp on the glue on these joints.

4.6 Motor Mount

The motor mount is very easy to make. I use craft sticks, which cost about a penny each. A small miter box and saw cut them easily.

I prefer to build the motor mount without any downthrust, although you will need about 3°. It's just too easy to get the motor mount out of alignment if you have to build it with funny angles.

4.6.1 Cut and Glue Pieces

All you need to do is build a square. Piece at the top, piece at the bottom, and two pieces for the sides. Size them to fit the motor and the fuselage. The structural glue works great with wood.

4 Building

4.6.2 Drill Holes

I predrill holes for the motor mount screws. These need to be smaller than the wood screws that come with the motor (see Figure 4.34 on the next page).

4.6.3 Glue on Fuselage

Glue the motor mount onto the fuselage using the structural glue. Important! Make sure that the motor mount is horizontal and flat against the fuselage. Funny angles here will make your model fly funny.

4.7 Final Assembly

4.7.1 Painting and Decorating

Consider decorating your model before before you glue the major components together (see Figures 4.36 on page 114 and 4.37 on page 115). It'll just be easier to do it now. Apply masking tape to the surfaces where the glue will go.

4.7.2 Glue on Wing and Horizontal Stabilizer

Carefully line up the wing and the horizontal stabilizer. It helps to weigh these down so they don't move.

Mark on the fuselage top where the structural glue needs to go. When you are ready, apply the glue and position the fuselage. Make sure it is at 90° to the wing and tail (see Figures 4.38 on page 116 and 4.39 on page 117).

Weigh down the fuselage some at the tail and wing. Be careful not to cause it to bend. The idea is to make sure there are no gaps in the glue and that the pieces will not move until they dry. Since these are large glue surfaces, wait one or two hours before moving it.

Figure 4.34 Motor Mount
The wider piece lines up with the top edge of the fuselage.

4 Building 113

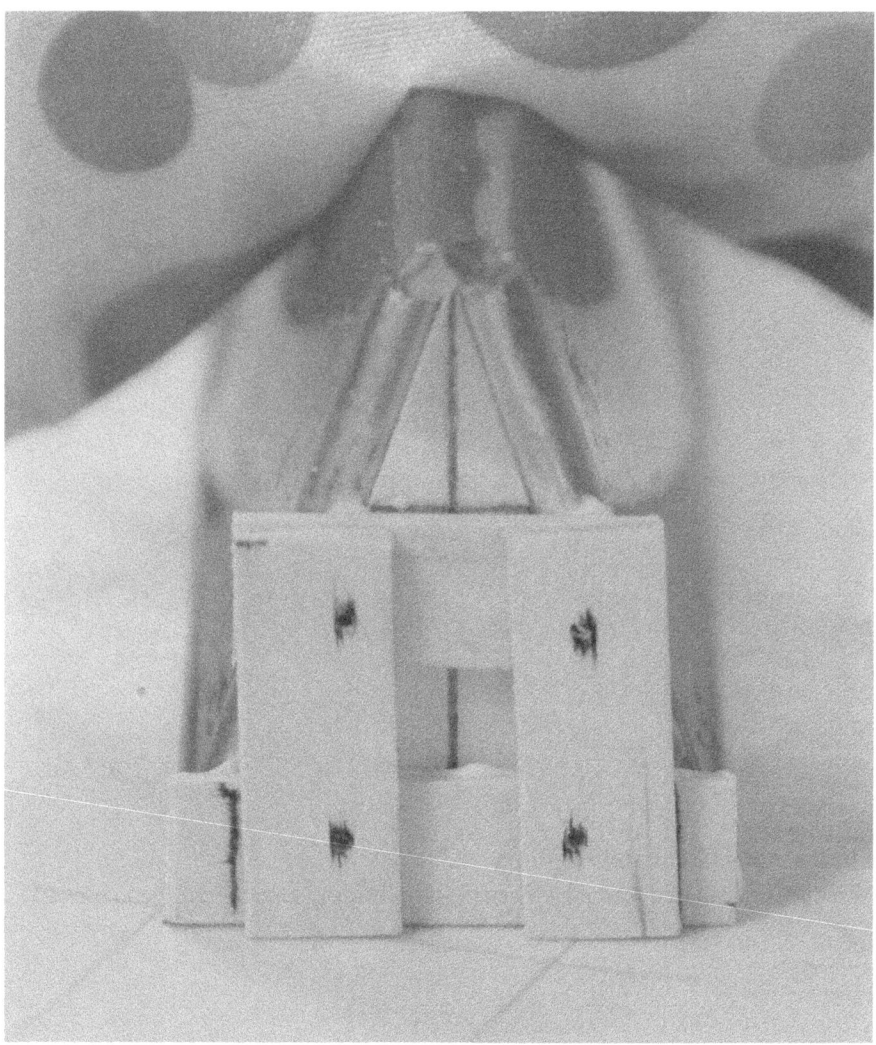

Figure 4.35 Motor Mount on Fuselage
Glue upside down so that the motor mount top lines up with the fuselage top.

Figure 4.36 Hand Painted Wing
With some practice and an airbrush, outstanding results can be achieved.

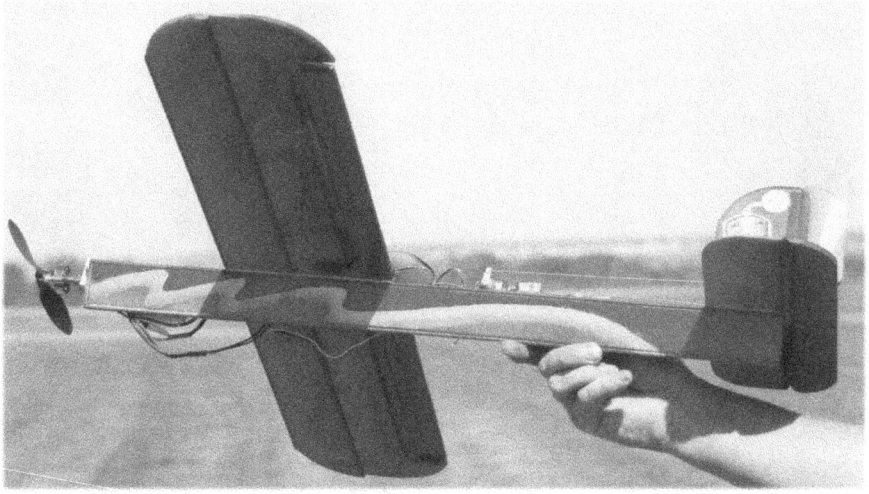

Figure 4.37 Hand Painted Fuselage
Even a simple pattern works great.

Figure 4.38 Glue on Wing and Horiz Stab
Only put weights directly over the wing and tail. It's better to put the control horns on after this step.

4 Building

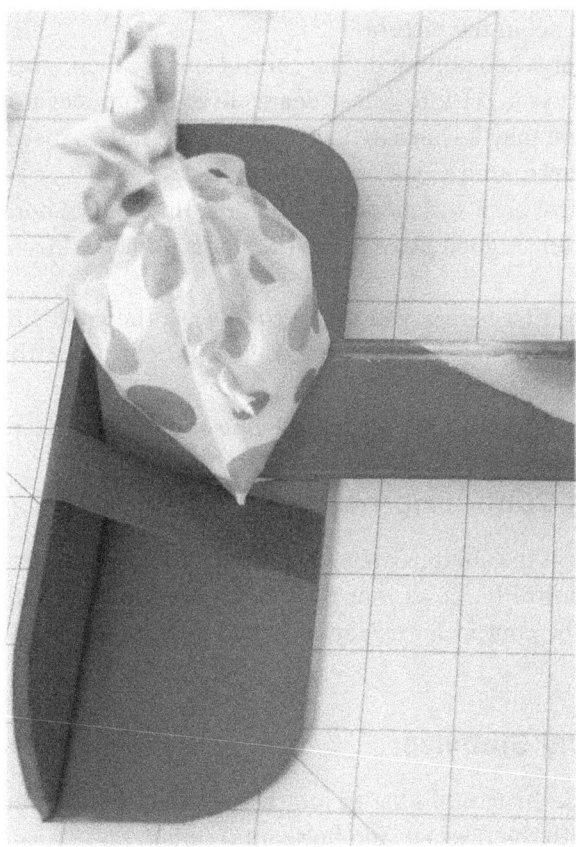

Figure 4.39 Glue on Horiz Stab
Closeup of tail.

4.7.3 Mount Elevator Control Horn

Waiting to glue on the elevator and aileron control horns will make it easier to glue the wing and horizontal stabilizer onto the fuselage. I forgot to do this while building the model in the pictures.

Control rods are stronger when pulling on the control surface than when pushing against it. When you get into a fast death dive, the up elevator command that can save you may be hard to do because of the fast airspeed. You want to pull on the control rod to get up elevator.

Cut the slot for the control horn and mount like before. This control horn will be on top of the elevator. A good place to cut the slot is $\frac{3}{4}$ inch out from the center of the elevator.

Test fit the control horn first before you glue it in place. The goal is to have the hole be right over the hinge line or right *behind* it, slightly over the elevator.

Once you are happy with it, take some structural glue and fix it in place.

4.7.4 Mount Aileron Control Horns

The airplane will fly better if the ailerons are symmetrical to each other. Try and mount the aileron control horns so that their holes are lined up with each other. I like to put the control horns about $\frac{3}{4}$ inch in from the inside edge of the ailerons.

4.7.5 Glue on Vertical Stabilizer

Flip the airplane over. Use structural glue to attach the vertical stabilizer. Make sure it's lined up with the fuselage and horizontal stabilizer.

4.7.6 Attach Motor

Use screws to attach the metal motor mount and motor. The motor wires should be on the right side of the airplane.

4 Building

You need some downthrust. One washer under each of the top two screws should do it (see Figure 4.40 on the following page). I've never felt the need for side thrust.

4.7.7 Attach Propeller

I use prop savers, which are black O rings, to hold my propellers to my motors. Sometimes an airplane lands and the propeller has disappeared. This is because the O ring broke in flight. Seems like a small price to pay for all the times it kept the propeller from breaking.

Always balance a new propeller. Most propellers are fine to begin with, but the loss in performance from an out of balance prop can really bite you.

4.8 Radio Installation

4.8.1 Tape on Tail Servos

The rudder and aileron servos are attached to the fuselage using double sided tape. Using tape is easy and works well.

The elevator servo faces to the right and the rudder servo will face to the left. If you put the rudder servo to the rear and the elevator servo to the front, you'll usually equalize the length of their connector wires.

Here's a trick. It's hard bending the piano wire so that you get exactly the length you need. To make the servo installation a lot easier, bend the piano wire *before* you tape down the servo. That way, the piano wire will always be the right length.

Aim to have a small gap between the two servos. Then even if the wire length comes out a little off, you'll still be fine.

I use a craft stick and small clamps to make sure the rudder and elevator are in the neutral position before I tape down the servos (see Figure 4.41 on page 121).

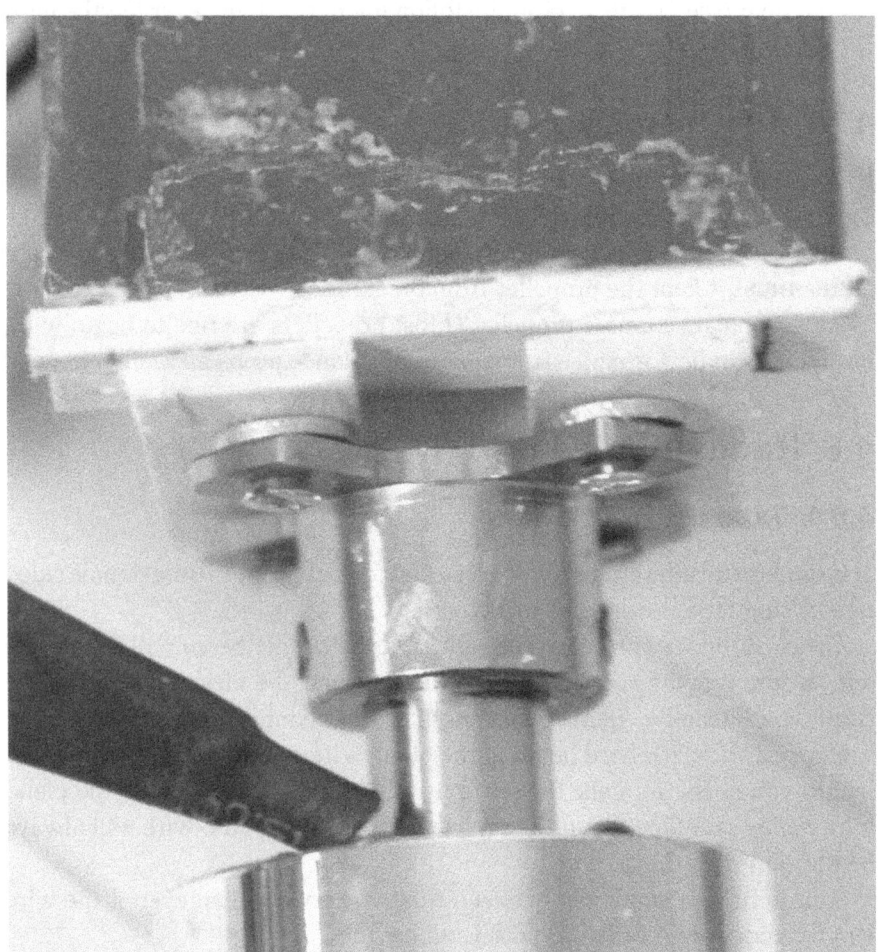

Figure 4.40 Motor Mount Washers
Top view of the motor mount. Use two washers under the top of the motor mount.

4 *Building* 121

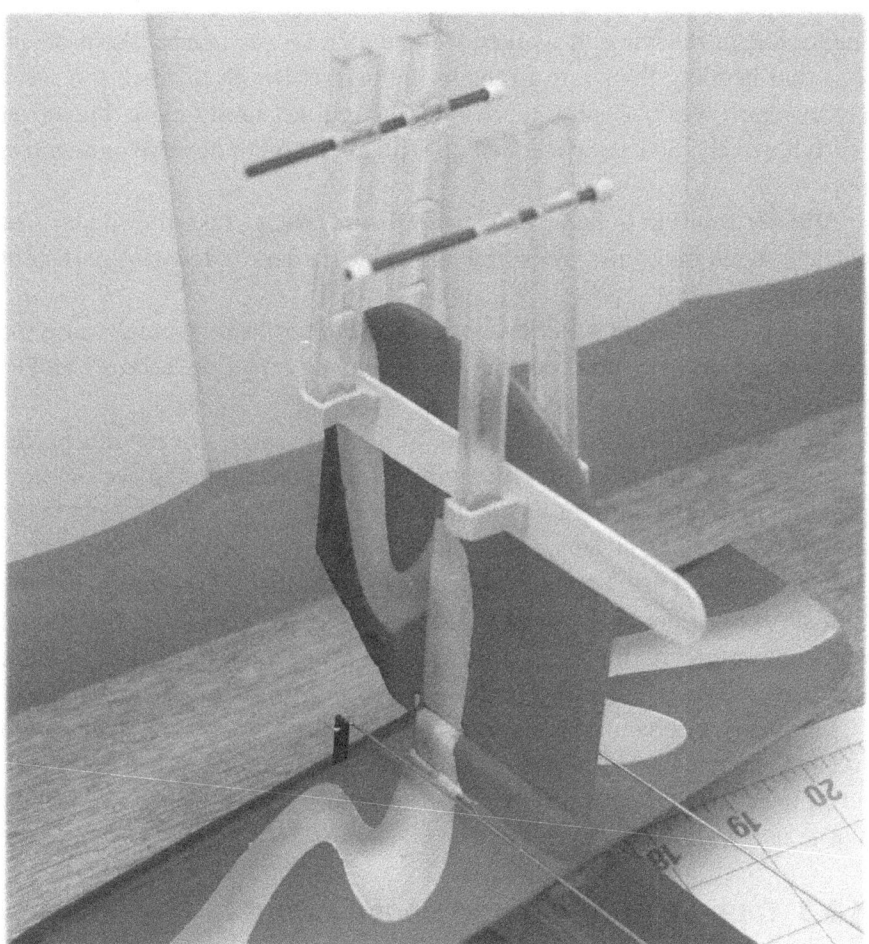

Figure 4.41 Taping Down Rudder Servo
Clamp down the rudder to make sure it's at neutral.

4.8.2 Tape on Aileron Servos

I built most of my prototypes with just one aileron servo stuck in a hole in the middle of the wing. It worked well enough for my needs. The problem was that bending the control rods to the perfect length to reach the servo control horn was basically impossible. I could get pretty close, but never reach it exactly. So I always ended up with a little bit of positive or negative flap.

A better solution is just to use two aileron servos. Like the rudder and elevator, bend the control rods *first*, then glue the servos down. A perfect fit everytime!

Use a craft stick and small clamps or some other means to make sure the ailerons are in the neutral position before taping down the servos (see Figure 4.42 on the facing page).

The obvious downside is the weight of the extra servo. It's not much. The advantages are many. Besides removing a tricky assembly step, we can now program in aileron differential and flaps. We also avoid cutting a hole in the middle of the wing, always a good thing.

Make sure you use the same model servo for both ailerons. I prefer to use four servos, all identical. Keeps it simple. Have the wires from the aileron servos meet up with the wires from the tail servos at the trailing edge of the wing (see Figure 4.36 on page 114).

The piano wire control rods for the ailerons are thicker than they need to be. But since they're so short, there's no significant weight penalty. The advantage is that we can use the left over piano wire from the tail servos. Waste not, want not.

4.8.3 Tape on Receiver and Speed Control

The receiver and speed control are mounted using double-sided tape. Easy (see Figure 4.43 on page 125).

When viewed from the rear, the propeller turns clockwise. This means that the fuselage has a tendency to turn counterclockwise because of propeller torque. To help counteract that tendency, mount the battery on the right

4 Building

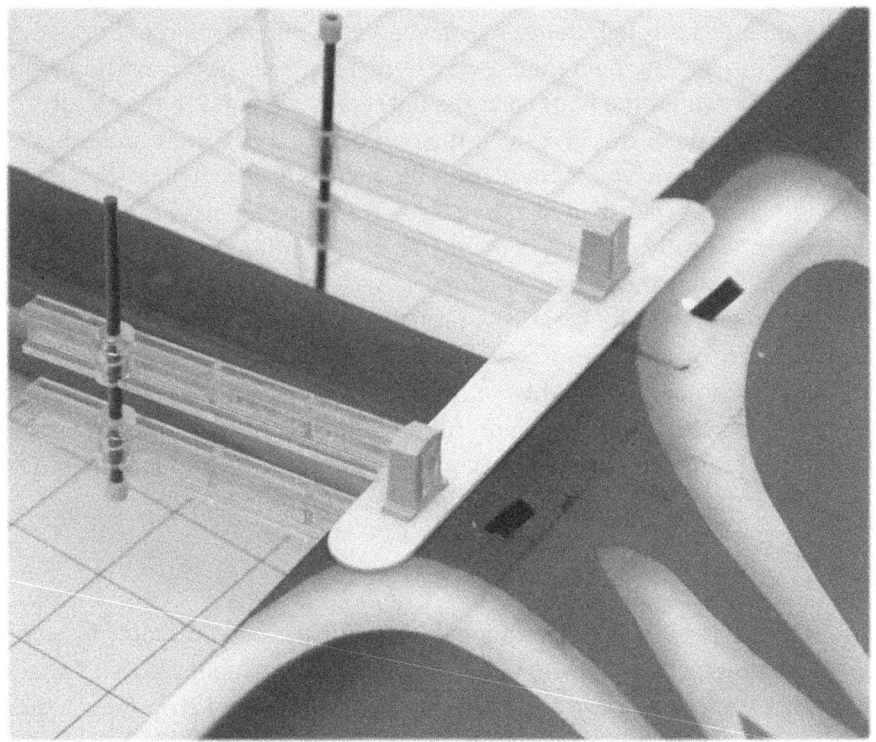

Figure 4.42 Taping Down Aileron Servos
Easy as pie.

side of the fuselage. Having a connector wire go under the bottom of the fuselage doesn't look right. So put the receiver and speed control on the same side as the battery.

Here's another trick. With a spread spectrum receiver, it is best if the antenna is pointing straight up. Just drill a small hole in the wing and stick one of the antennas through there. I've never seen a difference in performance, but if it bothers you, figure out a way to seal the hole. You can also mount the receiver behind the wing near the tail servos like I did in the picture.

If your speed control gives you the option, use a soft start and a brake. The soft start keeps you from tearing the motor off the mount. I've never seen this happen, but why take a chance. The propeller actually causes less drag when it's fully stopped than when it's windmilling.

I normally shut the motor off completely right before I touch the ground on a landing. With the brake, the propeller also stops moving right away. Lower chance of motor or propeller damage that way.

Braid the motor wires and twist the battery wires. At the very least, tape the wires together. This helps prevent an inductance build-up in the speed control that can eventually damage it. If you have to lengthen the wires, leave the battery wires alone. Lengthen the motor wires.

4.8.4 Velcro the Battery

Use the battery to balance the model. Aim for the balance point to be on the main spar or right in front of it. This is the only component that I attach using hook and loop fasteners (Velcro). Use a horizontal strip longer than what you need in case you fly with different-sized batteries like me.

4.8.5 Radio Programming

You want about $\frac{1}{8}$ inch up elevator when it's in neutral. The rudder and ailerons should be at zero degrees when neutral.

I'm not a fan of dual rates, but love exponential. I like to setup the control surfaces so that I get maximum deflection with full stick movement (about

4 Building 125

Figure 4.43 Radio Components
Since the paint job made my model a little tail heavy, I had to mount the battery pretty far forward. The speed control is under the wing's leading edge and the receiver is behind the wing.

45° for all of them), then add in about 30% exponential to tame the controls around neutral. If you want an even tamer model, 50% exponential is not out of the question.

If your transmitter does not have exponential, then setup your control surfaces so that they move about $\frac{1}{2}$ an inch in both directions.

Here's a radio programming trick. Find a spare switch on the transmitter and use a programmable mix to make the switch force the throttle to 0% power. You preferably want to use the same switch on all your models. The idea is to have a kill switch for the motor. Not much work for a nice safety feature.

The model flies fine without any fancy radio programming. But if you've got the capability, then go ahead and use it. You can have a lot of fun just fiddling with all the transmitter settings and then flying the supercharged model.

A small amount of throttle to elevator mixing helps with the need for downthrust. Be careful not to overdo this.

Aileron effectiveness when the power is off can be low. Reinforcing the ailerons helps a lot with this. Mix in some rudder into the aileron and all of a sudden it flies just great.

Aileron differential (more up aileron than down) should be a given. It lowers the need to use the rudder to coordinate the turns.

If you want to show off, you might as well program in some flaps. No, you definitely don't need them on a slow flying model like this one. But I won't stop you from trying to have some fun. Use 15° of flaps for takeoff. You can program in some elevator mixing to compensate for the down flaps. For tight loops, program in some flap deflection when the elevator is maxed out.

5 Flying

5.1 The Right Place and Time

I know that this is really hard to do, but try and resist the temptation to go out and do a maiden flight when the weather conditions are not optimal. Give the model a fighting chance by waiting until the winds are low.

Actually, winds are not really the problem. The real problem is gusts. A steady wind can actually help by getting the model up to flying speed sooner. But where I fly gusts are ever present when the wind is blowing.

I've gotten burned a few times by weather forecasts. The wind speed forecast does not take into account gusts. Not long ago, a forecast for 3 mph winds was accurate, but they had left out any mention of the 15 mph gusts.

You'll have better luck by flying in the early morning or late afternoon. Less likely to have other people around and the wind will be less, too.

You may be tempted to test fly it indoors because of the lack of wind. I don't recommend it because the ground will probably be harder and you'll usually have more space outside.

5.2 Preflight

Thoroughly check your model before you launch.

Grab every part of it and try to move it. Does it move more than you expected? Do you see any cracks or breaks anywhere? Is anything loose that shouldn't be?

I've gotten very good at predicting where an airplane will break. It's usually at the places where there is a concentration of stress in the structure.

These stress risers occur at joints and at places where a material has a sharp angle.

Here's a fun exercise for a rainy day. If you have an old model airplane that you don't think you'll want to fly again, try some destructive testing on it. Push it, pull it, bend it, and twist it. Watch carefully what happens. This is always a very educational exercise.

Sight along the fuselage and wing to check the alignment. An out of alignment model may be an indication of hidden damage.

Check the control surface movement direction and amount. Any binding? Any slop? If you have radio mixer settings, confirm that they work as expected.

Recheck the balance. It should never be behind the main spar.

Nudge the throttle forward to make sure the motor is turning in the right direction. Does anything look like it might shake loose?

Even if all you plan to do is a test toss, make sure your name, address, telephone number, and AMA number are on the model. You need most of this information on the model if you have to file an insurance claim with the AMA. Adding the words "Reward If Found", won't hurt, either.

Per the AMA Safety Code, you must also perform a radio equipment ground-range check before flying a new model. The conditions for a range check are determined by the radio manufacturer, but they are usually full radio control at 30 paces with reduced transmitter power output.

You might be able to put the model on the ground and do the range check by yourself if you can still see the control surfaces move at 30 paces. If you do this, somehow disable the motor before you start walking away.

5.3 Toss It

It'll be easier if a friend throws the model while you concentrate on the controls. A neckstrap helps a lot if you are doing both at the same time (see Figure 5.1 on the next page).

5 Flying

Figure 5.1 Launching
I like to handlaunch my models by matching their cruise speeds and angles of attack. They literally fly off my hand. Courtesy of Peter Jensen.

I've never seen tall grass here in Albuquerque. If I toss the model power off, it'll do a very short glide before it hits the ground. As a compromise, what I tend to do is run the motor but at reduced power. It's not enough power to make the model go wild if something is very wrong, but it works very nicely to stretch the glide. It gives me more time to react and to observe what it does. If I like how it glides, I usually nudge up the throttle so that it starts climbing.

Be careful with the comments of onlookers. They are two steps removed from the model (you are one step away). A model that looks unstable to them might just be the victim of a pilot that's nervous and all thumbs!

5.4 Repairs

For quick field repairs I suppose you could use foam safe CA and accelerator. It's very rare for me to break something so badly on this model that I cannot keep on flying.

The foam has a very pleasant organic quality to it. I once had a mid-air collision with a balsa airplane. My propeller cut through the plastic film covering and I got a two inch deep dent in one wing. This particular prototype had no leading edge dowel.

Well, the balsa airplane was grounded. The plastic film provides much of the strength of the wing, and with a cut through it the integrity of the wing was compromised. Me? I just folded back the jagged foam pieces and kept on flying. After I got home I put some structural glue in the break and that was that.

5.5 Extended Test Flying

After you're past the critical maiden flight and the model looks promising, test fly it at different locations under different weather conditions. Try a variety of flight maneuvers. Let others have a go at it. The idea is to develop a complete picture of the behavior of the model.

6 Enhancements

Before making major changes to the model, try making some relatively minor tweaks.

6.1 Painting and Decorating

Adding a color scheme is the safest modification you can make, since it should not affect the flying qualities. Just be careful and don't add too much weight. Since most of the surface area of the model is behind the CG, painting it all will shift the CG back.

I've never had a problem with XPS melting on me, but watch out for solvents in paints. The last thing you want to happen is for your completed model to melt as you decorate it as a finishing step. *Always* try it out on a scrap piece of foam first.

Krylon H2O spray paint cans are water based. Use masking tape and clear plastic wrap to cover the areas you don't want to paint. Frisket film is also used for this. The main problem with spray paint cans is that there is no easy way to control the mount of paint being deposited.

Art and craft stores carry water based paint markers. They are a bit pricey, but lay down a beautiful opaque line. These are made by Sharpie and others.

I also experimented with decorative papers. Rubber cement won't make them curl when you glue them down. In a pinch, a glue stick will work, too. You may want to use a clear protective spray as a finishing touch.

Broad tipped markers or felt-tipped pens work well enough. However, they are not opaque and need plenty of time to dry.

A great choice is acrylic paint. It's water based and there's a rainbow of colors available at craft stores for about a dollar a bottle. A couple of drops go a long way. Even better, it dries very quickly. Buy the opaque colors for better surface coverage. A fan brush works great to get rid of brush strokes.

Don't use tempera paint. It just flakes off after it dries.

Craft stores also carry a large selection of decorative stickers. These are made for the scrapbooking crowd.

For the best finish, nothing beats an airbrush. A decent airbrushing system will cost you about $100 and it takes some practice to get good at it. But once you do, you'll love the results.

The model pictured on the cover was hand-painted using an airbrush. It took about twice as long to paint it than it did to build it. The paint also added about 0.3 ounces (8.5 grams) to the total airplane weight. I was actually very surprised that the weight gain was so little, given the multiple coats of paint that it received. The result was truly beautiful, but it's really up to you to decide if the results are worth the effort.

One warning. Despite its solid appearance, foam is surprisingly translucent when sunlight is shining through it. It's not a good idea to only paint one side of the wing. The color will shine through to the other side and you'll have a hard time telling which side of the wing is facing you. This is especially true with dark opaque colors.

At a minimum, you need some way to tell the top of the wing from the bottom. More than once I've had test pilots give the transmitter back in a hurry because they got confused about which way was up on one of my unpainted models. When I was in a hurry, I made a few quick passes with a marker and I was done. Fluorescent orange, yellow, or green work great since they show through the wing less.

6.2 Removable Wing

I built a couple of models with removable wings. I didn't like how they came out, but the problems were fixable. The main challenge is making sure the dowels holding down the rubber bands are fixed securely to the fuselage.

6.3 Landing Gear

I always fly from grass when outdoors, so testing a landing gear is a challenge. I have to admit that I didn't want to include a landing gear in the basic model because that would give the impression that I thought it was necessary. I definitely don't feel that way. Keep it simple and leave it off unless you really want one.

Use a piece of piano wire to build it. Try wire 0.060 inches thick (1.5 mm). You may need thicker wire depending on the quality of your landings. It should be located near the leading edge of the wing. It needs to be long enough to keep the propeller from striking the ground when the fuselage is level. About five inches high should do it.

6.4 Sorta Scale

Decorating it to look like a Piper Cub is an easy one.

Giving the wing and tail different shapes is not hard. You just need a good imagination and the willingness to try it. Make sure their areas stay close to the same to maintain the nice flying qualities.

6.5 Camera Plane

I've flown the model with an extra battery pack attached. That is about the same weight as a micro photo/video camera. It flies fine.

You can handlaunch a small model like this from just about anywhere. That gives you access to many more interesting flying sites and photo opportunities than the typical field out in the middle of nowhere.

7 Variations

This is what you've been waiting for. Now that you know how to build and fly a stock version of the model, it's time to really start experimenting.

The stock model is capable of a wide range of aerobatic maneuvers. Either at my hands or that of others, I've seen it do high alpha, stalls, inside/outside loops, knife edge, inverted, slow flight, high speed, rolls, 3D hovering, and rolling circles. For such a simple model, that's quite a repertoire.

7.1 Free Flight Glider

Leave out the motor and radio system. Don't cut out the control surfaces. Attach pieces of heavy duty aluminum foil to use as control tabs. The model will weigh about half what it used to. You will need to add weight to the nose to balance it out. Rigging some sort of bungee launch system should not be hard. It'll be even easier to turn it into a towline glider.

If your budget is really tight, this is by far the least expensive option. Get in the air literally by spending just five bucks.

This is also a great option for a school-age kid. I'd say that a middle schooler is just about ideal. How about getting together a boy scout troop and building them as a group?

Learning how to fly a radio-controlled model airplane takes some practice. Building a free flight glider makes it a lot easier for a kid to be successful.

Another option is to create teams consisting of several kids and one experienced builder/pilot. Then the standard model could be built and the kids can still have active roles in the building phase.

7.2 Basic Trainer

The model is slow and stable enough for a beginner. It turns fine just from rudder input. You may want to leave out the ailerons to save a little bit on the weight and cost.

I'm tempted to recommend adding some polyhedral, but it probably doesn't need it.

7.3 Slow Flyer

For flying indoors, it needs to go as slowly as possible. Do everything you can to trim the weight. Use a 10 gram motor and a 350 mAh 2S battery. Leave out the ailerons. Leave out the wing leading edge dowel. Consider leaving out one or more of the fuselage support dowels.

7.4 Sloper

I've actually flown one of my prototypes on the slope. It was a lot of fun! Since the airfoil is so thin, it had no problem penetrating into the wind. If I got into trouble, I could just turn on the motor and fly back to a safe spot.

Feel free to build one without a motor. Beef up the wing spars. Setup some sort of ballast system. Velcro at the CG comes to mind.

Instead of using 1/8 inch dowels, use 3/16 inch ones instead. They will add some weight, but will make the structure ultra strong.

7.5 Combat

Why not? Attach a streamer and go at it. It won't get any cheaper than this.

Since maneuverability is so important, you may want to shorten the wings and increase the size of the ailerons.

7 Variations

A recent popular variation on combat is Last Man Standing. No streamers, just crash into the other guys and disable their airplanes. This is a perfect model for that.

7.6 Pylon Racer

Even better, make it a one class pylon racing event. That will even out the playing field. As with combat, make the wings smaller.

7.7 Motorglider

Extending the wingspan to increase the wing efficiency will be a challenge to do while minimizing the weight increase. Try doubling up the spars in the center section only.

Thin airfoils like the KFm1 are never going to be great soaring airfoils. The KFm3 airfoil (two steps on top) is a little bit more efficient. But you should be able to create a decent fun motorglider.

7.8 3D Aerobat

My model has been hovered by thumbs better than mine. The weight, size, and power-to-weight ratio is comparable to commercial 3D flyers. The only issue is that my model is not laid out symmetrically. It can do the maneuvers, just not as cleanly.

Moving the wing to the middle of the fuselage to a midwing location will take some design work. Most of my prototypes were built with flat vertical fuselages. Three layers of foam should be about right. Cut a hole in the middle and slide the wing in. It'll be a challenge making it strong enough.

A better fit for this type of model would be a KFm4 symmetrical airfoil.

8 Make It Your Own!

Low weight and high strength is the holy grail of airplane design. I like to joke with my friends that I managed to make my model so light and strong by leaving out a bunch of stuff that I just didn't need. Stuff like wing taper, washout, dihedral, wing sweep, wing incidence, tail incidence, carbon fiber, Kevlar, fiberglass, covering material, balsa, and spruce. I did manage to leave in easy building, great flying, and a healthy amount of crash resistance.

Don't make the mistake I made and try out too many new ideas at the same time. Building an unflyable model is a frustrating experience, even if you see it coming. One prototype, one major untested idea, please.

Make as few changes as possible at a time and keep the design as simple as possible. Designs invariably get more complex as they get test flown and tweaked. Try to at least start with a simple design. Find the core of the idea and strip everything else out.

Focus on building as light as possible with just enough strength. When something breaks and it shouldn't have, strengthen the part as necessary. This way you'll organically grow the strength of the model only where needed. Once in a while, step back and completely rethink the design.

Be adventurous! I had so many dismal failures only because I was willing to take a chance on wacky ideas. Sometimes the idea failed miserably, but opened the door to some other interesting ideas. I would never have arrived at the final design I did if I hadn't taken a lot of chances along the way.

Question your assumptions. There are a lot of well-meaning but misguided statements being made out there. Make sure you really understand why something is a certain way.

Have fun. Share what you've learned with others. When you have a design you are proud of, I'd love to hear about it.

Index

3D, 137
3M Durapore Surgical tape, 66

acrylic paint, 131
adhesives, 67
adverse yaw, 37
aerobatics, 137
aerodynamics, 32
aft CG, 35
aileron differential, 37, 124
aileron effectiveness, 36
ailerons, 48
airbrushing, 131
airfoil, 32, 37
airplane type constant, 46
Aleene's Tacky glue, 68
aliphatic resin glue, 68
anemometer, 56
angle gauge, 70
angles, 59
aspect ratio, 45

battery, 49
BEC, 50
bleeding edge technology, 30

Blenderm, 66
Blue Wonder, 49, 51
BlueCore, 39
building, 73

calculator, 51
caliper, 70
camera, 133
canard, 28
carbon rod, 28
CAs, 68, 130
Cellfoam 88, 39
clean release tape, 67
CNC foam cutter, 28
combat, 136
complex shapes, 59
constraints, 27
control horn, 66
control surfaces, 48
control throws, 124
Coroplast, 39
cost, 43
craft sticks, 49, 67
cruise, 53

cutting mat, 71
cyanoacrylates, 68

decorating, 131
decorative paper, 131
Depron, 39
design constraints, 27
design goals, 27
design process, 27
design requirements, 27
destructive testing, 127
dihedral, 35, 41
Dollar Tree, 63
double sided tape, 49
dowels, 32, 64
downthrust, 34, 37, 38, 49
drafting tape, 67
drag, 36
Dremel, 28, 70
drill press, 70
dual rates, 124
duct tape, 39

E-Z connector, 66
Eagle Tree logger, 56
easy to build, 28
efficiency, 51
elevator, 48
Elmer's Ultimate glue, 40
enhancements, 131
epoxy glue, 68
EPP, 39
EPS, 39

Ercoupe, 36
exponential, 124

field tools, 56
flaps, 124
flying, 127
flying location, 127
flying wing, 28
foam cutter, 28
foamboard, 31, 45, 47, 63
free flight, 28, 135
Frisket film, 131
fuselage, 47
fuselage side area, 41

glider, 28, 35, 135
glue safety, 69
glue stick, 67
glues, 67
goals, 27
Gorilla glue, 40
gusts, 127

H2O, 131
hardwood, 59
hardwood dowel, 32
hinge tape, 66
hobby knife, 69
hook and loop fastener, 40
horizontal stabilizer, 47
hot melt glue, 29
hot wire foam cutter, 28

incidence, 36

Index

indoor, 28, 31, 53
induced drag, 36
inexpensive, 29
initial design, 31
insulating foams, 39

Kadet 40, 46
KFm, 32
KFm1, 38, 45, 46
KFm2, 37, 46
Kline-Fogleman, 32
Krylon, 131
Kv, 50

laminating glue, 67
landing gear, 133
launching, 128
Liquid Nails Perfect Glue, 68
Liquid Nails Small Projects, 68

markers, 131
masking tape, 67
materials, 31, 63
miter box, 69
model size, 31
model stiffness, 37
motor, 49
motor mount, 49
motorglider, 28, 137
music wire, 65

Nexcare Durable Cloth tape, 66
nylon ties, 66

paint marker, 131

painter's tape, 67
painting, 131
paper airplane, 47
park flyer, 28, 31
ParkZone Vapor, 33, 51
performance, 30
piano wire, 49, 65
pilot skill level, 32
pin vise, 69
plywood, 39, 49
polypropylene, 39
polyurethane glue, 40, 68
power rule, 49
power system, 31, 49
PP, 39
preflight, 127
propeller, 49, 51
propeller balancer, 70
propeller torque, 122
prototyping, 32
pusher, 28
PVA, 68
pylon racing, 137

quiz, 34

radio programming, 124
radio system, 58
razor blade, 69
razor saw, 69
RCadvisor, 23, 51, 147
receiver antenna, 58
rejected ideas, 37

removable wing, 40, 132
repairing, 130
requirements, 27
Reynolds number, 32, 38, 45, 53
roll stability, 35
rotary tool, 28, 70
rudder, 48
rulers, 70

sanding stick, 70
saw, 69
scale, 70, 133
servos, 58
sexy looks, 30
Sharpie, 70, 131
Sig Kadet 40, 46
size, 31
slope glider, 28, 136
sloper, 28, 136
slow flyer, 28, 31, 40, 136
specifications, 59
speed control, 49
spray adhesive, 29
spread spectrum, 58
spruce, 32
stall, 36, 41, 46, 51, 55
stickers, 131
stiffness, 35, 37, 59
strapping tape, 39
strength, 59
stress risers, 127
structural components, 45
structural glue, 68

Sumo glue, 40
supplies, 63
sweep, 41

tachometer, 56
tail, 47
tail heavy, 35
taper, 41
tempera, 131
test flying, 33
test pilot, 58
thermals, 35
tools, 69
trainer, 28, 32, 40, 136
twist, 41

ungoals, 30

vacuum bagging, 28
Vapor, 33, 51
variations, 135
Velcro, 40
vertical stabilizer, 47
video camera, 133
voltmeter, 56

Walmart, 63
Weldbond, 68
wind, 127
wind speed meter, 56
wing, 45
wing dihedral, 41
wing incidence, 36
wing loading, 32

Index

wing span, 45
wing stiffness, 35
wing sweep, 41
wing taper, 41
wing twist, 41
winning design, 43

XPS, 39, 59, 63

yaw oscillations, 34

z bend, 49, 66
z bend pliers, 69

Colophon

About the Author

I founded www.RCadvisor.com in 2007. Born in Puerto Rico, I grew up in New York City.

I've had life-long love affairs with airplanes and computers. As a child, I built and flew many rubber-powered model airplanes. I then moved on to small gas control-line models. In the mid-90s I helped pioneer the electric revolution by flying a .40 size electric model. I hold a Private Pilot-Glider license and once owned a full-size AS-W 20 high performance sailplane. I'm currently very active in my local model airplane clubs, recently accepting the position of Vice President at one of them.

I've been a computer programmer all my life. I got my first personal computer in 1981 and got my first paid job as a computer programmer a couple of years later while still in high school. I graduated with a degree in computer science from Columbia University. I've also been a fan of aviation for as long as I can recall. While growing up, I always dreamed of becoming an airline pilot. I've been straddling these two fields my entire life.

RCadvisor's Calculator

Some of the website visitors are very curious about the story behind the calculator. Here is a summary of that story.

During the summer of 2007 I was putting together an electric power system for a new model airplane I had just purchased. I was very disappointed with the power system calculators available. It looked like the time was right for a shake-up in the model airplane calculator market. I've been working

Figure 8.1 Carlos Reyes

on it full-time since then. I don't have much time to go flying for fun right now!

I wrote the first version of the calculator using Dojo[1], a web browser AJAX toolkit which uses JavaScript. I liked how it was coming together, but ran into a problem when it came time to do the charts. You see, there are no good solutions for doing interactive graphics from JavaScript today. The best solution I found was a Flash chart control. It worked fine, but then I started thinking. Why not do the whole application using Flash?

I finally settled on Adobe Flex[2], a very powerful application framework. Flex is compiled and runs inside Flash. It looks great (see Figure 8.2 on the facing page)! I'm only using the open source core of Flex. Ironically, I ended up writing my own charting module. The calculator was at about 26,000 lines of source code the last time I checked. Flex is a very high-level computer programming language, so that actually is a lot of source code.

---

[1] www.dojotoolkit.org
[2] www.adobe.com/flex

Colophon

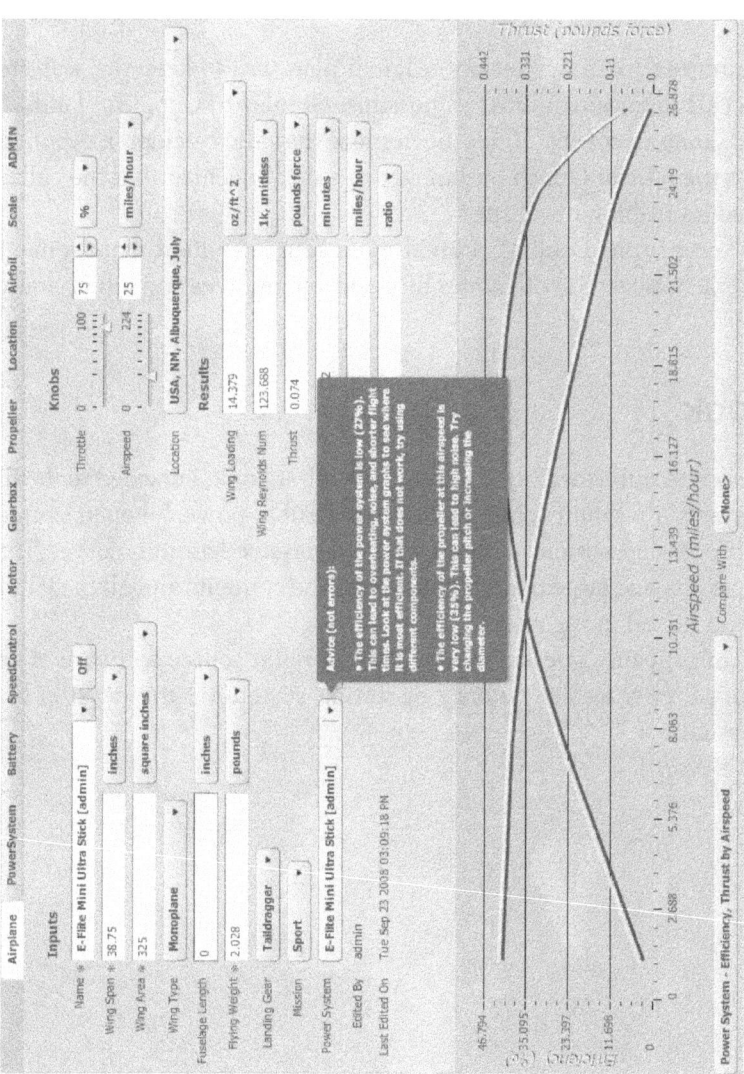

Figure 8.2 RCadvisor's calculator

Website

It sounds funny to me now, but my original plan was to keep the website around the calculator as minimal as possible. Similar to Google's[3] landing page, it was going to consist of not much more than the calculator. About a week before the official launch on January 1, 2008, I decided that the calculator merited a full-blown website.

The web server runs Drupal[4], a great open source content management system. I've customized it with about fifty add-on modules and much elbow grease.

This Book

This is my second published book. As with my first book, I decided to do all the work myself. I wrote it using LaTeX, an incredibly powerful open source document processing system with an equally massive learning curve. The entire book is just one large plain text file with the contents and all the LaTeX commands all mixed in together.

As you can probably guess, I'm a big fan of open source software. I've been running Linux[5] as the primary operating system on my desktop for several years now.

Regrets? Never.

---

[3] www.google.com
[4] www.drupal.org
[5] www.linux.org

www.ingramcontent.com/pod-product-compliance
Lightning Source LLC
LaVergne TN
LVHW061216060426
835507LV00016B/1958